P9-CLO-063

*Thomas Jefferson
Selected Writings*

Crofts Classics

GENERAL EDITOR

Samuel H. Beer, *Harvard University*

Thomas Jefferson
Selected Writings

EDITED BY

Harvey C. Mansfield, Jr.

HARVARD UNIVERSITY

Harlan Davidson, Inc.
Wheeling, Illinois 60090-6000

Copyright © 1979
Harlan Davidson, Inc.
All rights reserved

Except as permitted under United States copyright law, no part of this
publication may be reproduced or distributed in any form or by any means,
or stored in a database or any retrieval system, without prior written
permission of the publisher. Address inquiries to Harlan Davidson, Inc., 773
Glenn Avenue, Wheeling, Illinois, 60090-6000.

Visit us on the World Wide Web at www.harlandavison.com

Library of Congress Cataloging-in-Publication Data

Jefferson, Thomas, 1743–1826.
  Selected Writings.

  (Crofts classics)
  Reprint. Originally published: Arlington Heights, Ill.
  AHM Pub. Corp. ©1979
  Bibliography: p.
1. United States—Politics and government—1783–1809. 2 Virginia—
Politics and government—1775–1865. 3. United States—Politics and
government—Revolution, 1775–1783. 4. Jefferson, Thomas, 1743–1826.
I. Mansfield, Harvey Claflin, 1932–. II Title.
E302.J442   1987   973.4'6'0924   87-6703
ISBN 0-88295-120-3 (pbk.)

Manufactured in the United States of America
06 05 04 03 14 15 16 17 CM

contents

introduction   vii

principal dates in the life of Thomas Jefferson   xliii

A Summary View of the Rights of British America
(excerpts)   1

The Declaration of Independence   7

Two Letters on the Declaration
      To Henry Lee, May 8, 1825   11
      To Roger C. Weightman, June 24, 1826   12

An Act for Establishing Religious Freedom   13

Notes on the State of Virginia (excerpts)
      Query VI: Productions Mineral, Vegetable and
      Animal   15
      Query VII: Population   26
      Query XI: Aborigines   28
      Query XIII: Constitution   28
      Query XIV: Laws   36
      Query XVII: Religion   46
      Query XVIII: Manners   50
      Query XIX: Manufactures   52
      Query XXII: Public Revenue and Expenses   53

Draft of the Kentucky Resolutions   55

First Inaugural Address   62

A Selection of Letters
       To James Madison, January 30, 1787   67
       To James Madison, December 20, 1787   68
       To James Madison, March 15, 1789   72
       To John Adams, June 27, 1813   74
       To John Adams, October 28, 1813   75
       To Thomas Law, June 13, 1814   79
       To Pierre Samuel Dupont de Nemours,
       April 24, 1816   81
       To John Taylor, May 28, 1816   83
       To Issac H. Tiffany, August 26, 1816   87
       To Samuel Kercheval, July 12, 1816   88
       To John Holmes, April 22, 1820   91

selected bibliography   93

introduction

> All honor to Jefferson—to the man who, in the con-
> crete pressure of a struggle for national independence
> by a single people, had the coolness, forecast and ca-
> pacity to introduce into a merely revolutionary docu-
> ment, an abstract truth, applicable to all men and all
> times. . . .

> Mr. Jefferson . . . was, is, and perhaps will continue to
> be, the most distinguished politician of our history.

These two judgments of Abraham Lincoln on Thomas
Jefferson, the one praising him for giving a national struggle
the dignity of a human struggle, and the other suggesting his
partisan skill, may be considered to set the problem of Jefferson's political thought. As the author of the Declaration of
Independence, Jefferson made himself one of his country's
Founders as well as one of mankind's benefactors, though
he was not present at the Constitutional Convention and
hence was not one of the "Framers." Yet he was also a
supreme partisan. He fought three remarkable adversaries,
John Adams, Alexander Hamilton and John Marshall, in
contests so stirring that historians today still cannot describe
them dispassionately; he founded the oldest political party
in the United States; and beyond this, he founded the very
institution of partisanship, party government, which settled
into the two-party system we maintain today. Why did Jefferson decide that the "abstract truth" must be sustained in a
party or that the party must promote an abstract truth?

The Declaration of Independence

The "abstract truth" Lincoln meant was the "self-evident
truth" of the Declaration of Independence that "all men are

created equal." Jefferson was the author of the Declaration, but he wrote it at the behest of a committee and for the approval of an assembly. He said later that its authority rests on "the harmonizing sentiments of the day," not on any "originality of principle or sentiment."[1] The Declaration cannot be taken simply as an expression of Jefferson's own political thought because he was speaking in the name of a nation. Yet it was the very basis of his partisan career too. In the 1790s he formed his Republican party to recover the principles of the Declaration and to inspire the country with the revolutionary fire of its signers. It is an uncanny fact that Jefferson (and John Adams) died on the fiftieth anniversary of the signing of the Declaration.

If the Declaration harmonized the sentiments of the day (Jefferson specified that he meant the *Whig* sentiments, favorable to independence from Britain), it was not therefore merely in harmony with those times. Lincoln's praise was for something more, and the phrase "self-evident truth" did not mean a truth then thought obvious. A self-evident truth may be obvious or obscure, but it must contain its meaning within its own terms rather than look to something outside. To see that all crows are black one must look at crows, but to understand what "all men are created equal" means one must know only the meaning of "man." This is said to be a "truth," be it noted. It is not a concept created by men, for men have themselves been created. Men must make their way in a world and be guided by a truth they have not made. Since their freedom is based on this truth, they are not free to deny it. Nor may they regard this truth as an ideal to be aimed at, for it states the real nature of man from which, and by which men must build. What, then, can be found in the "self-evident truth" that all men are created equal?

The Declaration is not a proclamation from a superior chosen people. Its object, Jefferson said later, was to present "an appeal to the tribunal of the world" and it implies, as the document itself says, a "decent respect to the opinions of mankind."[2] Although it also appeals to the "Supreme Judge" for the rectitude of its intentions, its addressee is

[1]Letter to Henry Lee, May 8, 1825. *The Writings of Thomas Jefferson,* ed. P. L. Ford. Vol. 10, p. 343. Hereafter cited as *Writings.*
[2]*Writings,* vol. 10, p. 343.

chiefly the present generation of human beings, who are created equal. Since they are equal, they hold unalienable rights to life, liberty and the pursuit of happiness; for nobody can reasonably yield or alienate these fundamental rights to his equal, or justly ask his equal to alienate them to him. But the rights by themselves are not secure. Though they cannot be alienated to rulers who rule by the favor of nature or the grace of God, they can only with difficulty be limited and made consistent with each other. It appears that government is required as much when men are held to be equal as when they are held to be unequal, and government must get obedience by consent in the first case when it could ask for deference in the second.

To secure these rights, governments derive their just powers from the consent of the governed, and when "any form of government becomes destructive of these ends, it is the Right of the people to alter or abolish it, and to institute new Government. . . ." Americans, however, could not institute a new government without dissolving the political bands that had connected them to the British people, under the King of Great Britain; so the right of consent to government became, for them, the right to independence. But every people must have begun with the need to assert this right against other peoples. Every *man* is equal to every other man, and so every *people* is entitled to a "separate and equal station" among the powers of the earth. This consequence is by no means obvious, for it requires a shift from individuals to societies. Men are created equal, but the equality of peoples among the powers of the earth is achieved and protected by the right of men to govern themselves by consent. Equality among societies means independence, and this is a Declaration of Independence. Men are created equal, but they are divided in consequence of this equality into independent peoples. If men did not need government, their equality would not force them to divide themselves into independent peoples who must defend themselves against each other in war and revolution. One must not forget that the Declaration was a statement of reasons for going to war. The equality of men, therefore, has special reference to government: men are equal both in the lack of natural or divinely-appointed rulers and in the need for government.

Thus the Declaration is not chiefly concerned either with the form of government or with defining individual rights against the government. Clearly, men have rights against the government, which the British government had violated in America. But to secure their rights, men must use government as a weapon against offending governments, and so they need it just as much as they must fear it. Liberty is presented in the Declaration not so much in the familiar problem of a free individual versus a free government as it is in the people's right to alter or abolish, and institute, *any* form of government, as long as it rests on consent. In *A Summary View of the Rights of British America*, a proposed statement of instructions to Virginia delegates to the Continental Congress in 1774, Jefferson had said: "From the nature of things, every society must at all times possess within itself the sovereign powers of legislation."[3] The foundation of liberty is the supremacy of the legislative power; and this supremacy is understood not merely as a principle of internal organization but chiefly as the reason for the divisions of human beings into independent peoples. It is through political organization that men are united into a people, and by virtue of their union, divided from other peoples.

That all men are created equal is a "self-evident truth," is explained and defended at length in the political philosophy of John Locke. The Declaration, moreover, implies without saying explicitly that men live as individuals in a state of nature where they have no political relations before they make themselves a people by consenting to government. A "people," it seems, cannot exist except as the consequence of its own political decision, for the American people, though heretofore "connected" to the British, was connected to them by its own consent and hence potentially independent. Yet the necessity to infer a prepolitical state of nature in the principles of the Declaration reveals the importance of politics in that document. It sees obligation in the decision of a people and in men as members of a people, not in unconnected individuals. The reason for this is surely in the circumstances of the Declaration, which describe a people in colonial dependency rather than the state of nature. But it is interesting that the same liberal principles we usu-

---

[3] *The Papers of Thomas Jefferson*, ed. J. P. Boyd. Vol. 1, p. 132. Hereafter cited as *Papers*.

ally see used to protect individuals against government here defend one people against another people by instituting a government against their government. These circumstances, as we recognize today, are not so rare as they may have seemed to defenders of liberalism writing about established liberal societies. The political philosophy of liberalism is not so incapable in the problem of founding as some of its detractors, and defenders, have assumed.

The Declaration implies that a people is made and can make itself by means of a political act. In this it differs from the doctrine of modern nationalism, which tries to make political divisions conform to pre-existing nations defined according to culture or language. In *A Summary View*, Jefferson said that Americans, like the Saxon ancestors of the British, had used their natural right of "departing from the country in which chance, not choice, has placed them, of going in quest of new habitations, and of there establishing new societies, under such laws and regulations as to them shall seem most likely to promote public happiness."[4] Politics need not be ruled by chance—by the fate of birth in nations; on the contrary, nations—Jefferson usually says "peoples"—can be built by men aware of their natural rights and alive to an opportunity of exercising them. Jefferson was not a nationalist, not even a liberal nationalist. If he had been, he might have had doubts about the justice of displacing the Indian nations in America. Slavery he knew was wrong because it denied the unalienable rights of man, but for this reason, the culture of primitive peoples ignorant of natural right did not deserve respect. Jefferson studied Indian languages because of his interest in the origins of man. He was not a nationalist, but neither was he an internationalist who believes that national differences can be overcome or transcended. For Jefferson, national differences are essentially *political* differences, and mankind is irremediably divided because human liberty takes effect only in the independence of one people from another. If men were divided merely by the accident of birth in different cultures, one might hope for the institution of international organization by the operation of human choice. But in the Declaration, it is precisely human choice in politics that divides men.

[4]*Papers*, vol. 1, p. 121.

The element of choice in the making of a people is given emphasis in the "patient sufferance" of the American people. "Mankind," the Declaration says, "are more inclined to suffer, while evils are sufferable, than to right themselves by abolishing the forms to which they are accustomed." In the present case, the American colonies have endured "a history of repeated injuries and usurpations," and it is to prove this that the Declaration recites "a long train of abuses and usurpations" by George III. Mankind are slow to anger, and in their deliberateness there is opportunity for deliberation. The Americans show they have in fact made a deliberate choice by submitting facts to a candid world. Their "decent respect to the opinions of mankind" keeps them not merely to a standard of morality, but also to a rough standard of prudence in proceeding slowly and perhaps choosing carefully. Government by consent means government by choice rather than whimsy, at least or especially in the fundamental act of making an independent people. In this attempt to make government by consent seem moderate or even wise, Jefferson and his cosigners indicate that government by consent requires a measure of moderation and wisdom in those consenting. A people does not have a right of self-determination merely because it constitutes a separate nation or culture, nor is it likely to make itself independent hastily and regardless of circumstances. Nevertheless, it does have a right of self-determination merely because it may constitute a separate people; and the right of consent is more securely fixed to the nature of man, which is equality, than is the wisdom of those consenting.

Choosing to have a government and hence to be a people comes before the choice of any particular form of government. The Declaration specifies that governments derive their just powers by consent, but it does not specify which governments do that best. It does not even rule out any forms of government, though absolute monarchy seems to be rejected by implication. Limited monarchy, however, such as the then existing British government, is apparently included among governments that *could* gain the consent of a people. Otherwise it would have made no sense to list "a long train of abuses and usurpations" in the longest part of the Declaration; it would have been enough to say that monarchy is illegitimate in itself. Apparently all governments must rule by consent, but there is some leeway not only in the details of free government but even in the character or form of the government as a whole. This conclusion, which admittedly we must infer from the Declaration, must be reconciled with the fact that the party Jefferson formed later based itself on "republican principles" and could find nothing more damning to call its opponents than "monarchists." Moreover, the Declaration does not require representative democracy as we practice it today. Specifically, equality in consent does not necessarily imply "one man, one vote," for the former is *the* principle on which free government is founded, while the latter is *a* principle on which it may operate. Jefferson, it may be noted, changed his mind about "one man, one vote"; at first he opposed it, and later favored it. He never wavered in his adherence to the view, apparently indifferent to forms of government, that all government be by consent of the governed.

So much for the strictly political meaning of the self-evident truth that all men are created equal; it does not require democracy and it does require independent peoples. Thus far, however, we have not mentioned the meaning Jefferson himself (as opposed to his cosigners) thought most important. Writing just before his death, he called the Declaration a signal to arouse men to burst the chains of "monkish ignorance and superstition." This, and not "the present King of Great Britain," is cited as the real enemy. Jefferson explained why in memorable words: "All eyes are opened, or opening, to the rights of man. The general spread of the light of science has already laid open to every view the palpable truth that the mass of mankind has not been born with saddles on their backs, nor a favored few booted and spurred, ready to ride them legitimately, *by the grace of God.*"[5]

In this quotation politics and religion are inseparable. A certain religious belief, called "monkish ignorance and superstition," induces men to hold that some men are better than others because they are favored with the grace of God. Holding this political consequence of their religious belief, they give their consent to governments that do not respect

[5]Letter to Roger C. Weightman, June 24, 1826, *Writings*, vol. 10, pp. 391–92. The italics are mine.

the rights of man. They use their right of consent unwisely. The Declaration, therefore, is by no means neutral on religion, but it judges religion by its political consequences, that is, by its conformity to the self-evident truth—the equality of men. Every people, says the Declaration, has a separate and equal station among the powers of the earth by virtue of "the Laws of Nature and of Nature's God." A belief in Nature's God, it seems, is compatible with, or reinforces (but does not seem necessary to) respect for human equality.

"Nature's God" was intended in contrast to a revealed god; so the Declaration (at least in Jefferson's understanding) seems hostile to revealed religion. Revealed religion is revealed only to the godly, and from what Jefferson said in many places against priests, one may suppose that the godly will take advantage of the favor of revelation to demand political power for themselves or their allies. Revelation in its nature, and not merely by its abuse, is opposed to the equality of men. On the other hand, "the light of science" is open to man as man and also teaches the equality of men. Of course Jefferson never made himself a crusading deist like Tom Paine; he accommodated himself to a mild Christianity, and tried to make it still milder by compiling a renovated gospel entitled "The Life and Morals of Jesus of Nazareth." As we shall see, he thought that to secure the rights of man, the people must believe either in a revealed religion made harmless to those rights or in Nature's God. But he always promoted the authority of science over the authority of revealed religion. He was himself a scientist in his spare time, making inventions, conceiving explanations, and corresponding with other scientists. Yet though he was greatly interested in science, he was, as a political man, still more interested in the *authority* of science, for he felt that science as opposed to revealed religion supports the vital self-evident truth of human life.

Judged politically, science and natural religion support the equality of man, while revealed religion opposes it. It follows that government which respects the equality of man must secure the support of science and natural religion, while rendering revealed religion harmless. This it can do by separating the churches of revealed religion from the state, for priests cannot then make alliances with governments in which rulers receive divine favor and priests earthly privileges. Because religion and politics are inseparable, church and state ought to be separated. Because free government cannot be indifferent to the character of religion in a free society, it ought to be neutral among the churches of revealed religion.

Thus the Declaration would, after all, discriminate among forms of government to this extent: no government could respect the rights of man if it maintained an established (revealed) religion. But with this inference we go well beyond what the Declaration says explicitly. It does not mention the separation of church and state and does not reproach George III for maintaining an established religion in any of the colonies. Jefferson at this time was beginning his attack on the establishment of the Church of England in Virginia. In one of his bills on disestablishment (offered to the General Assembly of Virginia in 1776), he asserts that a change in form of government makes necessary corresponding changes in laws, since some are "founded on principles heterogeneous to the republican spirit. . . ."[6] This would justify the inference we have made, with Jefferson's suggestion, from the Declaration. But it is safe to say that few who signed the Declaration considered its main intent to attack "monkish ignorance and superstition." This was Jefferson's own gloss, and one may add, a partisan gloss. Jefferson had to fight long and hard for complete disestablishment in Virginia against "Whigs" (that is, partisans of American independence) who did not agree that the self-evident truth of human equality demands separation of church and state. The Declaration harmonized sentiments of the day in favor of independence, but its apparent indifference to forms of government left ground for party conflict over the political consequences of its central, self-evident truth.

Notes on Virginia: Natural Resources

Jefferson was a one-book author, and his one book, *Notes on Virginia,* was written in the period 1780–1784 during and after his brief tenure as Governor of Virginia. *Notes on Virginia* consists of "queries" put by "a Foreigner of Distinc-

[6]*Papers,* vol. 1, p. 562.

tion," Francois Marbois, seeking information about America, which Jefferson, through an intermediary, undertook to answer. Thus Jefferson caused his one book to appear as answers to questions in private rather than a voluntary offering to the public. The full title is *Notes on the State of Virginia.* "State" means "condition" as well as "government," and the book contains facts relating to the condition of "Virginia," especially its power among nations in the 1780s and its future potentiality for such power. In the eighteenth century, the term "statistics" was used with a wider meaning than quantitative facts to describe the state of power in a country.

Now this country was of course America, not merely Virginia. Marbois had asked for information about all the states, but Jefferson chose to tell about America through these *Notes on Virginia.* Though in the first Query he gives the exact boundaries of Virginia (then much larger than now) as they were determined by charters and grants from England, he goes on in the second Query to describe all the principal rivers in America westward to the Mississippi. It is as if he wished to indicate how powerless the Old World was to set limits to the New World. Many of his statistics (including the kinds of quadrupeds and of Indians or "aborigines") refer to America rather than Virginia, and his comment shifts with ease from remarks on Virginia to thoughts on America. Perhaps he means to use the meaning of the name, "Virginia." As John Locke once said ". . . in the beginning all the *World* was America," so now Jefferson seems to say America is Virginia, a virgin land in which mankind can make a new beginning.

The *Notes on Virginia* can then be seen as Jefferson's own justification for the Declaration of Independence. Now that the *right* of the American people to independence has been established, their *capability* for independence must be demonstrated. If America were permanently inferior to the Old World, its right to independence would be reduced to an actual subordination. It would be like a newly freed colony in our day that had no basis for independence either in natural resources or in national pride and unity. A former colony lacking the basis for independence can easily become a colony again in fact if not in name. A "declaration" of independence, therefore, is not enough; it must be backed

by a proof that this people, the American people, can sustain
its independence against nature and against foreign powers.

These two enemies of a people's independence, nature
and foreign powers, are taken up separately in *Notes on Virginia*. The first eleven "Queries" (i.e., chapters) concern the
natural environment of Virginia and America; they try to
prove, at the least, that contrary to the views of certain
French natural philosophers, and to the prejudices of most
Europeans, nature has not enlisted herself as a partisan of
Europe. The last eleven Queries take up the political and
cultural state of America, the conventional environment
created by man, and show that America does not suffer from
cultural dependence or from what is today called
"neocolonialism." The Twelfth Query on counties and
towns provides the transition from the natural to the conventional state of the country, for Jefferson there discusses
the relative power of nature (by means of rivers) and the
laws to decide the existence and importance of towns.[7]

America has natural power in its self-sufficiency. The first
eleven Queries show that the New World is not lacking in
any natural resource. It has an extensive and well-connected
system of rivers, and no seaports other than the mouths of
its rivers. Thus America is neither forced nor encouraged by
nature to have commerce with the Old World; it can trade
with itself. Nor does it need "productions, mineral, vegetable, and animal" from the Old World, for all can be found
in this "extensive country." America has the temperance
and variety of climate to support a civilized and independent
society. It has a population growing fast enough to double
itself every twenty-seven years, and hence has no need of
emigrants from the absolute monarchies of Europe, who
bring with them either the principles of such governments
or their extreme contrary, an "unbounded licentiousness."
Even though labor, not land, is scarce in America, Jefferson
suggests that it is better to wait patiently for an internal
growth that will produce a people "more homogeneous,
more peaceable, more durable." This reasoning applies
more strongly to the importation of slaves, which has been

[7] I am indebted for this observation to Jane Johnson Benardete.
Marbois had put 22 queries, but Jefferson made them 23 and
changed their order; *Papers*, vol. 4, p. 166.

prohibited "while the minds of our citizens may be ripening for a complete emancipation of human nature."[8]

True to his division of the subject into the natural and cultural environment of America, Jefferson discusses the Indians, not slaves, in the first part of the *Notes on Virginia.* They are called "aborigines" as the inhabitants found in America, not brought there; they have manners rather than laws and they use their natural moral sense of right and wrong in place of government. Though they live "principally on the spontaneous productions of nature," they are, again contrary to the view of the Count de Buffon, as brave, enduring, affectionate, sensitive, sexually potent and keen of mind as "Homo sapiens Europaeus."[9] They are, moreover, apparently older than "the red men of Asia," a conclusion Jefferson reached by a calculation of the antiquity of their languages. The American aborigines would then be among the aborigines of mankind.

The Indian stock, developed in America, is as good as European stock. It is in no way stunted as if the Indian were living on a second-rate continent. Perhaps this is why Jefferson (in the sixth Query) chose an Indian chief, Logan, to represent "the Man of America" and in the name of the New World to speak defiance to an English colonial governor, Lord Dunmore. Although Logan had long been a friend of the white man, his family was murdered by a white man, and in revenge he led his tribe to war. After it was defeated, Logan sent a speech worthy of Demosthenes and Cicero (Jefferson says) to Lord Dunmore. "There runs not a drop of my blood in the veins of any living creature," Logan asserted; and having "glutted my vengeance" for the injuries of one man, he now consents and rejoices that his country lives in peace.

Logan is an independent man because he has no ties to other human beings and because he can send his tribe to war on a mission of personal revenge. Jefferson admires his unlettered eloquence, but he also notes that Indians are barbarians for whom force is right. They have a natural moral

[8]Thomas Jefferson, *Notes on the State of Virginia,* ed. William Peden, pp. 85, 87. Hereafter cited as *NV.*
[9]*NV,* pp. 62, 96.

sense of right and wrong, but they do not know how to apply this in politics to the construction of civilized societies.[10] Logan, in his independence, shows no respect for the self-evident truths that all men are created equal and that government should be by consent of the governed. Natural or aboriginal independence is barbaric; it derives from the power of one's endowments, such as strength or eloquence, and of one's circumstances, such as the resources of the American continent.

The American people has received from nature a golden opportunity for building an independent nation, contrary to the prejudices of Europeans, but Jefferson did not wish to base his case for independence on that fact alone. The "Man of America" is "both aboriginal and emigrant." The emigrant American, as distinguished from the aborigine, has brought his understanding of civil government and natural right from Europe and perfected it on his own. With this great advantage, however, he suffers the great disadvantage of having ties with Europe. His independence is more civilized but more problematic. He cannot claim, in regard to culture, manners and beliefs, that he has no ties with "any living creature." George Washington, Benjamin Franklin, and David Rittenhouse are the examples Jefferson uses to show that America has contributed its full share of geniuses to the present age, but they must admit comparison to European geniuses and acknowledge an indebtedness to European civilization. They do not have the natural (though savage) independence of Logan: Jefferson himself had to argue the viability of American independence to the French philosophers and other doubters; he could not merely assert it as could Logan.

If Logan speaks for the American Indian, his fate may also be representative. After fierce resistance, he succumbed to the civilized but unjust conqueror, the emigrant American. This American, suppressing the memory of original immoral deed, must make his independence with a "new political science" (to anticipate the phrase of Alexis de Tocqueville) suited to his natural opportunity and directed to the reform of his cultural inheritance.

[10]*NV*, pp. 60, 93, 142.

Notes on Virginia: Reform

"Human nature is the same on every side of the Atlantic," whatever the greater bounty of nature in land and rivers on this side.[11] The more important difference between the Old World and the New is made by man, for, despite the advantages in natural resources and the equality of human nature, the aborigine is of course far inferior in civilization to both the European and the emigrant American. Now the superiority of the last, according to Jefferson, lay in his very understanding that all men are created equal. When men are understood to be naturally equal, their differences in civilization are attributed to their own striving and making (given the opportunity). But to understand civilization as chiefly man-made, which implies the power of human creation, is a keen incentive to make it better: hence the superiority of those peoples who believe in reform. The power of reform depends on the belief in reform.

Jefferson, it can be said with emphasis, believed in reform, and in this book he tried to teach the American people to do likewise. In the first part of the book, on America's natural state, no proposal for reform can be found, except for a brief discussion of Albino Negroes, who might be taken jokingly for nature's (inadequate) solution to the race problem. But when Jefferson begins to discuss human convention, he urges reform. He no sooner describes the constitution of Virginia in the first Query of the second part than he gives its six major defects and proposes a convention to fix it. Excusing the Virginia constitution, he says it "was formed when we were new and unexperienced in the science of government."[12] That was in 1776; ten years later he thinks "we"—his fellow Virginians—have achieved maturity in the science of government.

Jefferson's belief in reform is focussed on government. He begins the second part of his book by considering the constitution, and political science seems to be the key science for human improvement. The reason is the connection between human improvement and human equality. To repeat: re-

[11]*NV*, p. 121.
[12]*NV*, pp. 118, 129.

form has its full power only when every difference of progress, in a situation of equal opportunity, is attributed to human making; and this requires that men be held naturally equal. The first task of government, then, is to establish and protect the self-evident truth of human equality. To do this, it must secure, in a constitution, the rights of man that follow from the equality of man. Since the constitution of government protects the very possibility of reform, it has, or should have, a special status in a society dedicated to reform. It should not be "alterable by the ordinary legislature." The ordinary legislature can alter the laws, not the constitution; so the belief in reform dictates a distinction between the constitution and the laws.

Jefferson takes up "laws" in the next Query after "constitution" to indicate the *second* task of government, which is to serve as the agent of reform. Before government can reform effectually, it must be set on the only basis that can sustain reform over time, a constitution unalterable by itself. Government can reform the laws on condition that it not be allowed to reform itself, although it may propose constitutional reform.

The people make the constitution under which the government makes ordinary laws. In the rush of revolutionary conflict, Virginia's constitution was not made and ratified by delegates of the people selected for that purpose, and it shows the bad effects of making a constitution by the ordinary method of making laws. The majority is unrepresented in the legislature; the representation of those who do vote is very unequal; the Senate is composed in the same way as the House of Delegates; too much power is concentrated in the legislative body; and the ordinary legislature may alter the constitution itself. The people properly instructed would never have made such a constitution, which is indeed not really a constitution.

For Jefferson, politics is the crucial, but not the ultimate factor in society. The constitution protects the rights of man, but since the people make the constitution, it is they who ultimately protect those rights. The people are "the only safe depositaries" of government. Yet the people do not govern directly; they govern by elections through a constitution. Moreover, under this constitution, the government makes laws that affect the character of the people. To be safe depositaries of government, Jefferson says that even the people must be *rendered* safe; they are not so when uneducated or corrupted.[13] By means of the distinction between constitution and laws, the people govern and are made fit to govern. By enforcing respect for equality, they make reform possible; and yet by not governing directly themselves, they make it possible for the government to reform the people. Thus even the reformer is reformed. The trick of this recipe for progress is a constitution that is made by men but does not in the ordinary way seem alterable by them. The constitution is a convention above all ordinary conventions by which they may be reformed. It is surely not fixed for a long time, as Jefferson gave each generation the right—even the duty—to make its own fundamental convention. But the constitution must be made with a broader consent than the ordinary laws and on an occasion specially marked for fundamental change.

Jefferson's political science combines two ways of understanding politics that are often thought to be antithetical, the institutional and the sociological. He insists on a special status for the institutions in the constitution, while he also sees them in the context of the interests and manners in society that affect government. But the special status of governmental institutions is connected to a comprehensive social outlook, and for Jefferson the two ways of understanding politics are really one. Institutions must be kept fixed to secure the people's liberties against the ambition of a few, and society must be made republican to protect the people's liberties against their own carelessness and lack of vigilance. Only a republican people can remain free, but only a republican government with a fixed constitution can make the people republican.

Jefferson did not favor unending reform for the purpose of keeping pace with social change. His political science was in the tradition of Montesquieu. In his view politics has a function between the formative power of the Aristotelian regime and the reactive conciliator of social forces argued by modern political sociology. Government derives from the people, where it is "deposited," and yet acts on the people to keep them independent by making them republican.

An independent people must have a republican adminis-

[13] *NV,* p. 148.

tration of justice, and Jefferson proposed a revised code for
Virginia based on the common law of England but with
significant alterations from the existing body of British stat-
utes. Among these was a bill to abolish the importation of
slaves, to which was added an amendment to emancipate all
slaves, educate them, and send them elsewhere in colonies.
The bill with this amendment was too radical to succeed, but
the occasion gave Jefferson a chance to consider the problem of race in this book. Granted that all men are *naturally*
equal, can racial differences among them be disregarded in
the *conventions* of human societies? Arguing against the in-
corporation of blacks into the state, Jefferson seems to conclude (with some recent theorists of black power) that the
difference between black and white is too great to be kept
in one free and independent people. It does not follow,
then, from human equality that men can be equal members
of a racially mixed society.[14] For this unhappy conclusion
Jefferson gives political, physical, and moral reasons.

Political reasons can be found in the very injustice of
slavery: the "deep-rooted prejudices entertained by the
whites," and "ten thousand recollections, by the blacks, of
the injuries they have sustained." These are sufficient to
"divide us into parties, and produce convulsions which will
probably never end but in the extermination of the one or
the other race."[15] But Jefferson postpones this matter and
moves to "physical and moral" considerations.

First among these is the difference of color "fixed in nature" which makes the Negro less beautiful than the white
and unable to express his passions by changing color. In
addition, the Negro has an inferior mind: an equal memory,
but a much inferior reason scarcely capable, for example, of
comprehending Euclid, and a dull imagination. To substantiate this judgment Jefferson compares the literary works of
American black slaves with those of the Roman slaves who
lived in greater misery but excelled in the arts and sciences.
In the "endowments of the head," then, nature has been less
bountiful to the black. In justice and loyalty, however, the
black is fully equal; he steals when he does only because
everything is stolen from him. This clear difference of color
and supposed difference of faculty (Jefferson offers his opin-

[14] *Writings*, vol. 1, p. 68.
[15] *NV*, p. 138.

ion of the Negro's mental inferiority "with great diffidence") make it unthinkable in America to mix freed slaves and former masters, even if both should overcome their hatred and distrust of the other.[16] On the other hand, these differences do not justify slavery and do not permit America to perpetuate it indefinitely.

Another factor in the European inheritance is religion, and this also raises the problem of homogeneity in a free people. While men are held apart by the artificial institution of slavery, they are forced together by the establishment of religion. Jefferson fought the establishment of the Anglican church in Virginia for a decade, 1776–1786, in the "severest contests" in which he had ever been engaged. His "Bill for Establishing Religious Freedom," passed in 1786 in modified form, was in his opinion one of the three most notable works of his life, along with the Declaration of Independence and the founding of the University of Virginia. In *Notes on Virginia,* he supports religious freedom with the argument contained in this famous passage: ". . . it does me no injury for my neighbor to say there are twenty gods, or no god. It neither picks my pocket nor breaks my leg." Government can coerce "the acts of the body," not "the operations of the mind," because its legitimate concern is with what is injurious to the body, or by extension, to the purse. When government tries to extend its control to "the operations of the mind," it will establish an error, such as the view that the earth is "as flat as a trencher." If error is undesirable, so is uniformity of opinion; for it prevents the different sects from censoring each other's morals and by repeated persecution succeeds in no more than making "half the world fools, and the other half hypocrites."[17]

This is the argument of Locke's *Essay on Toleration,* and that work reserves the same exception: "the operations of the mind" may have to be coerced in order to protect toleration. Jefferson says, "Difference of opinion is advantageous in religion"; and to this he adds that difference of opinion is harmless in physics and geometry.[18] He does *not* say this

[16] *NV,* pp. 142–43.
[17] *NV,* pp. 159–60; *Writings,* vol. 1, p. 53.
[18] *NV,* p. 160; *Papers,* vol. 2, p. 546.

of political opinions regarding fundamental principles, the rights of man. Indeed, Jefferson did not regard the rights of man as being founded on mere opinion incapable of demonstration or liable to supercession; they are self-evident truths good for all time. By virtue of these rights, men consent to government to protect their life, liberty, and property from injury, and not to improve their souls. If this truth were but an opinion, it could not protect free inquiry into other opinions. The claim of a tyrannical government to abridge religious freedom (or to justify slavery) would stand equally with the demand for religious freedom as a matter of opinion, and the issue would be decided by force, not reason. It seems that civil rights must be defended against religious persecution by *established* political truths; so Jefferson composed a bill for *establishing* religious freedom. Such establishment may not require suppression of error, for reason will defeat error when free to combat it, but the government must instruct the people in their rights.

Moreover, it appears that government, while protecting religious freedom, must favor religion over irreligion. Jefferson agrees that the testimony of the atheist be rejected in a court of law: "reject it then, and be the stigma on him." Then, in a striking return to the political aspect of slavery, he exclaims:

> And can the liberties of a nation be thought secure when we have removed their only firm basis, a conviction in the minds of the people that these liberties are of the gift of God? That they are not to be violated but with his wrath? Indeed I tremble for my country when I reflect that God is just.[19]

In a warm climate no man will work who can get a slave to work for him; so in this situation liberty and economic interest are opposed. To overcome the opposition of economic interest, Jefferson implies, liberty needs the support of a religion that professes faith in a just God, benevolent but wrathful. Without such support, Jefferson could not reasonably hope for a total emancipation of slaves by the consent of their masters. This religion seems to be a Judeo-Christian monotheism rendered harmless to liberty

[19] *NV*, pp. 159, 163.

by the device of keeping it divided among many sects, whose disputes can be silenced if government takes no notice of them.[20] Religious freedom consists of an established sectarianism in which the necessary minimum of religion receives the support of government in public education and the unwelcome superfluity meets with contempt, fair argument, and ridicule. For the sake of liberty, government must support religion in general, but no particular religion.

Although this religion will clearly be predominantly Christian in America, Jefferson quotes from a pagan condemnation of slavery, and nothing from the Bible, in *Notes on Virginia*. In the natural (or theoretical) part of the book he says regarding natural or Biblical hypotheses: "he is less remote from the truth who believes nothing than he who believes what is wrong." (Query 6.) But in the corresponding Query 18 of the political (or practical) part, he says that it is necessary for the people to believe.[21] Religion has a status something like the status of the constitution: as the government needs a constitution above the ordinary laws to check its own ambition, the people need a superhuman source for their natural rights to force them to extend those rights to others when it is against their interest to do so. Jefferson apparently entertained doubts about the truth even of natural religion, but he was willing to use the strength of religion for political purposes. He said: "Truth can stand by itself." This seems to say that truth does not need the support of government. It may mean, however, that government gets its strength from the true rights of man, not the reverse. Then truth uses the strength of government as support when it is opposed by interest. Unwelcome restrictions and unpleasant duties will remain in the new world of the rights of man, and to secure them Jefferson resorted, in his own way, to the traditional method of finding or making a law above law.

Still another problem of human contrivance is education. Nature, we have seen, has provided America with her share of genius, but men of genius do not show themselves by nature. They must be elicited from the people through a

[20]*NV*, p. 161.
[21]*NV*, p. 33. Query 18 is on "manners," following Query 17 on "religion."

system of public education by which "the best geniuses will be raked from the rubbish annually...."[22] America must give opportunity to all, because nature has distributed talents among the poor as liberally as among the rich; but in giving favor, it must distinguish between "genius" and "rubbish," so that America can make the best use of its endowment.

This elitist statement of Jefferson's recalls another still more famous, in an exchange of letters with John Adams: "May we not even say that that form of government is best which provides the most effectually for a pure selection of these natural aristoi into the offices of government?" "These natural aristoi" are members of the "natural aristocracy" of virtue and talents as opposed to the "artificial aristocracy founded on wealth and birth."[23] They were confused together when the artificial aristocracy characteristic of the Old World was imported to the New, and the problem is to separate them. Jefferson proudly mentions in this letter that laws drawn by himself in the Virginia Revisal abolished entail and primogeniture, "the root of Pseudo-aristocracy." The best way to select the natural aristoi is by the method of free election by the citizens, who will not be corrupted by wealth or blinded by ambition. Yet the people must receive an elementary education and their minds stored, not with the Bible, but with morality and "the most useful facts" of history. History, especially, will make the people "safe . . . guardians of their own liberty," as it teaches them "to know ambition under every disguise it may assume" and to be jealous and suspicious toward their rulers.[24]

Education thus has the double purpose of enabling the people to distinguish the virtuous and the talented from the merely ambitious and of drawing the former from the main body of the people so that they can be prepared for promotion. In nature, men are created equal; in society, their inequalities come to the fore. Jefferson was no democrat in the traditional sense of the term, meaning a partisan of "rule of

---

[22]*NV*, p. 146.
[23]Letter to John Adams, October 28, 1813, *The Adams-Jefferson Letters*, vol. 2, pp. 388–89. Hereafter cited as *AJ*.
[24]*NV*, p. 148.

the people." He was willing to trust the people, not to govern, but to choose their governors. Being uncorrupt, the people will, if well instructed, choose the best and reject those who are merely well off; but as they do so, they constitute a kind of impartial judge separated from those whom they judge, who govern them. Their governors are drawn from them in a system of public education that gathers the best geniuses, but in the same act takes these best geniuses away from them. The people, then, are consoled for the loss of their natural equality partly by the principle of equality of opportunity. If they cannot govern themselves, they can be governed by natural aristocrats of popular origin, chosen by themselves—by the men who later were called "Jeffersonians."

These men get a "liberal education" in the Greek and Latin classics as well as in the sciences to make them guardians of the people's liberty. Their virtue is based on the natural moral sense Jefferson thought was in all men, which consists of helping others. They do not have special aristocratic virtues not found in all men, which might distinguish them and make them eager to distinguish themselves. Jefferson, though a zestful partisan in politics, frowned upon men of ambition. Ambition is a desire to excel in the virtues that raise a few men above the many, and Jefferson wished to use the aristocratic desire to excel in a rivalry to help and defend the people. His natural aristocracy, separated from the people by the system of education, looks back to the needs of the people; the principle of equality of opportunity serves the natural equality of man. He supported that aristocracy which serves the people, and serves them in a cheerful spirit of progress, not with gloomy condescension. He expected, however, that the aristocrats would become corrupt when they governed. His faith in education was limited by his faith in constitutions and elections, which in turn was limited by his faith in revolutions.

Aristocrats are promoted from the people so that they may use their talents for the sake of the people, rather than because they deserve a higher place to use their better talents for the excellence that only they can achieve. This distinction between a utilitarian and an intrinsic view of aristocracy may seem fine, but it allowed Jefferson to retain his belief in the self-evident truth of human equality in the face of many seeming violations of it in the society he helped to found, and enabled him to turn those inequalities to the account of human equality. He may have been guilty of overconfidence to think that public education can so easily find the natural aristocracy and control it, once found.

How should America provide for itself? "The political economists of Europe" were agreed that every state should establish its own manufactures, but the European inheritance, as before, could not answer the question for America. America had a special opportunity from nature, the resources for self-sufficiency and the rivers for internal trade as we have seen, but most important "an immensity of land." Unlike Europe where land was no longer available to support surplus populations, America was so big that it could choose whether to do its own manufacturing. And since America could choose, no doubt existed about how it should choose:

> Those who labor in the earth are the chosen people of God, if ever he had a chosen people, whose breasts he has made his peculiar deposit for substantial and genuine virtue. . . . Corruption of morals in the mass of cultivators is a phenomenon of which no age or nation has furnished an example.[25]

The economic question yields to the problem, both moral and political, of keeping a people free. Those who manufacture depend on "the casualties and caprices of their customers," and being dependent, become subservient and venal and live as "the mobs of great cities." Farmers, on the other hand, depend on themselves and on heaven, but not on other men. Their occupation makes the independent character of a free man, and hence of a free people. Instead of the variety of interests found favorable to freedom by *The Federalist*, Jefferson proposed that the farming interest be advanced over the others. He favored a variety of sects, but not of interests, and as we have seen in him immigration policy, he desired a homogeneous people. It was not as if America would have to do without manufactures, for the damage comes from making, not from having, them. "Let

[25] *NV*, pp. 164–65.

our workshops remain in Europe": This will keep Europe weak and corrupt, and America will have the best of both worlds.

Since foreign commerce must make up for the lack of manufacturing, America will not be self-sufficient. It must give up the natural independence allowed by its situation and resources for the sake of moral and political independence. Jefferson later accepted domestic manufacturing when American independence seemed to be endangered by the lack of it, but both views show that he understood a complex truth uncommonly well: that men in remaking their environment remake themselves. Technological progress, therefore, may have unforeseen and untoward moral consequences even in a site so favorable as America, and it is necessary to accept backwardness and dependency in manufacturing in order to protect the cultivated independence of free men. There is more than a hint of Rousseau's *Discourse on the Arts and Sciences* in this exclamation in a letter to John Adams: "And *if* science produces no better fruits than tyranny, murder, rapine and destitution of national morality, I would rather wish our country to be ignorant, honest and estimable as our neighboring savages are."[26] Today we may have to consider Jefferson's praise of the independent farmer as obsolete, but we have reason to share the doubts about the moral and political benefits of scientific progress which were the basis of his praise.

America has "an immensity of land." This means it has enough *new* land so that, in a rising population, every man can have a farm. But how much is enough for this purpose? Jefferson, we have seen, planned for a *rising* population (not merely for the contingency of a surplus) and he nowhere fixed an upper limit beyond which it should not rise. Will not this population need more land? America should remain a society of farmers "while we have land to labor," Jefferson says, clearly asking this question for himself. He seems to have recognized that when an independent people forsakes self-sufficiency, it must seek ways of expansion, not to satisfy an aggressive lust but simply to preserve its own freedom. Jefferson once called America "an Empire of liberty"; he did

[26]Letter to John Adams, January 21, 1812, *AJ*, vol. 2, p. 291; cf. vol. 2, pp. 332, 458.

so when as governor of Virginia in 1780 he commanded
George Rogers Clark to undertake an expedition to Detroit
from which, among other things, he hoped to "add to the
Empire of liberty an extensive and fertile Country thereby
converting dangerous Enemies into valuable friends."[27]
With the need for new land in mind, one can understand
Jefferson's concern for laws to limit speculation in land. One
can also appreciate the overriding motive for his Louisiana
Purchase. As so often happens with land, as happened in the
case of land bought from the Indians (which Jefferson himself noted), the buyer took advantage of the seller's distress.
In the need for new land as understood by Jefferson and
later by Jackson, one can see a strong motive for American
expansionism from 1780 to 1860.[28]

Such are the problems of founding an independent people on the basis of human equality. In regard to slavery,
religion, education, and economics it is not sufficient simply
to announce the self-evident truth as if its meaning were
clear. Even when all believe in human equality, so that Jefferson could assert that the Declaration merely harmonized the
sentiments of the day, the meaning of equality is arguable.
Notes on Virginia is agreed to be a major work of American
political thought, but this is partly for lack of many better
works and partly for the eminence of its author. It is in fact
a major work, comprehensive and carefully written. In it can
be seen every element of Jefferson's later political thought
(which appears only in speeches and letters) except his partisanship and the doctrine of states' rights, an instrument of
his partisanship. But even Jefferson's party is anticipated in
the program of reform he offers for Virginia and America in
the *Notes.* Its second part (Queries 13–23) constitutes a commentary of partisan interpretation on the facts of the natural
"state of Virginia" given in the first part. We must try to
understand why Jefferson thought himself justified in head-
ing a party to establish these reforms.

[27]Letter to George Rogers Clark, December 25, 1780; *Papers,* vol.
4, pp. 237–38. See Julian P. Boyd, "Thomas Jefferson's Empire of
Liberty," *Thomas Jefferson: A Profile,* ed. Merrill D. Peterson,
pp. 189–93.
[28]Harry V. Jaffa, "Agrarian Virtue and Republican Freedom,"
Equality and Liberty, pp. 59–66.

The Republican Party

For all the zeal and success of Jefferson's party, it is sur-
prisingly difficult to discover the chief points of difference
with its Federalist opponent, and thus the reason for its
existence. It is difficult not because the party was secretive
about its aims, but because the announced differences,
summed up in the title of the "Republican" party, are difficult to take seriously. Jefferson, though not a framer of the
Constitution, was not an Antifederalist opponent of it; he
claimed that the republican principles of his party were the
"true principles" of the Constitution.[29] As described in *The
Federalist* (a book that Jefferson said was "in my opinion, the
best commentary on the principles of government which
ever was written"[30]), the Constitution establishes an entirely
new kind of popular government. It is not the popular government of "the petty republics of Greece and Italy" in
ancient times, where the people ruled directly over a city. It
is modern representative government based on the rights of
all men, not just the many, and extended to the breadth of
a nation or empire. Yet it is neither the absolute monarchy
favored by Hobbes nor the limited monarchy preferred by
Locke, the two founding theorists of modern representative
government. It is republican, and unlike previous republics
that were steadied with hereditary aristocratic or monarchical elements, this republic is to be *completely* popular, its
checks and balances contrived entirely by institutions
elected or otherwise drawn from the people, with no admix-
ture, however limited, of hereditary monarchy and aristocracy.

On this general conclusion, Jefferson and his opponents
were agreed. If there was so much agreement on so much
innovation, what then remained to divide them? At the time
of the debate over ratification of the Constitution, Jefferson
had only two objections. He thought, as did many others,
that the Constitution needed a declaration of rights; and this
defect was soon remedied by the passage of the first ten

[29]Letter to Edmund Pendleton, February 14, 1799, *Writings,* vol.
7, p. 355; Letter to John Adams, June 27, 1813, *AJ,* vol. 2, p. 335.
[30]Letter to James Madison, November 18, 1788, *Writings,* vol.
5, p. 53.

amendments. But he also objected to the indefinite eligibility of the president for reelection. He thought that a president, once elected, could contrive his own reelection indefinitely, and so the provision of reeligibility would actually result in an elective monarchy for life.

That this result could occur, or that it would be harmful if it did, seems an unreasoning fear on Jefferson's part, and has usually been taken for such by historians. Yet he felt this fear, and we must make sense of it if we are to understand his party, its principles, and its career. Though after Washington's retirement Jefferson relaxed his belief that the Constitution must prevent the reelection of a president, he described his opponents as "monocrats" and asserted that the Constitution had been "interpreted and administered" like a *"monarchie masquée."*[31] Monarchy was not a casual or temporary danger to him, and to indicate his opposition, he called his party "republican." Why was he so fearful of "monarchy"?

Moreover, since Jefferson was so fearful, why did he tolerate any element of monarchy in the Constitution? For the president, by his own comparison, is an elective monarchy, whether for life or for one term. If he had been motivated by a phobia or exaggerated hatred of the British monarchy, he would have favored abolishing the king altogether, as did the "classical republicans" of the seventeenth century, Sidney and Harrington. Instead, following Locke and Montesquieu, he allowed a limited monarchy to be reestablished in America under the name of the "executive power," and he both considered and rejected the possibility of a plural executive.[32] He also would not have praised the British Constitution as the best existing constitution prior to those made by the American colonies, if he had been simply frightened of monarchy.[33] Nor, if he had merely hated the British, would he have asserted that Newton, Bacon, and Locke were the three greatest men who ever lived.

As Jefferson's views on monarchy seem to be the cause of

[31]Letter to Robert R. Livingston, December 14, 1800, *Writings,* vol. 7, p. 464.
[32]Letter to Destutt de Tracy, January 26, 1811, *Writings,* vol. 9, pp. 306–08; Letter to Marquis de Lafayette, November 4, 1823, *Writings,* vol. 10, p. 280.
[33]Letter to John Adams, September 28, 1787, *AJ,* vol. 1, p. 199.

his partisanship and the source of his party, they may perhaps be explained by referring to his views on parties. He never collected those views; but he had many occasions and ample time to compose them, for he was rightly accused of having infused American politics with higher party spirit than the Framers thought desirable or even tolerable. What could he say in defense? In letters to Adams after his retirement from the presidency, he began with a premise of considerable scope: "The same political parties which now agitate the U. S. have existed thro' all time ... in fact the terms whig and tory belong to natural, as well as to civil, history. They denote the temper and constitution of mind of different individuals." By such differences of mind, men form different opinions and by virtue of these opinions divide into parties "in all governments where they have been permitted freely to think and to speak." Jefferson also said that "one of the questions" dividing his Republican party from the Federalists was "on the improvability of the human mind, in science, in ethics, in government etc." But this opinion, which would yield a division into liberal or progressive and conservative parties, does not seem to be responsible for (though it characterizes) the *Republican* party and its opponent. The decisive difference of opinion is a difference about government, whether "the power of the people, or that of the aristoi should prevail."[34]

The difference over who should rule has always agitated free societies, but in describing the American parties Jefferson used significantly altered expressions, and did so consistently on several occasions.

Where a constitution, like ours, wears a mixed aspect of monarchy & republicanism, its citizens will naturally divide into two classes of sentiment, according as their tone of body or of mind, their habits, connections & callings, induce them to wish to strengthen either the monarchial or the republican features of the constitution.[35] (1797)

[34]Letters to John Adams, June 15, 1813, June 27, 1813, *AJ*, vol. 2, pp. 332, 335.
[35]Letter to James Sullivan, February 9, 1797, *Writings*, vol. 7, p. 117.

Both of our political parties . . . agree conscientiously
in the same object, the public good: but they differ
essentially in what they deem the means of promoting
that good. One side believes it best done by one composition of the governing powers, the other by a
different one. One fears most the ignorance of the
people; the other the selfishness of rulers independent
of them.[36] (1804)

. . . we broke into two parties, each wishing to give a
different direction to the government; the one to
strengthen the most popular branch, the others the
more permanent branches, and to extend their permanence.[37] (1813)

The line of division now is the preservation of State
rights as reserved in the constitution, or by strained
constructions of that instrument, to merge all into a
consolidated government. The tories are for strength-
ening the executive and general Government; the
whigs cherish the representative branch, and the
rights reserved by the States, as the bulwark against
consolidation, which must immediately generate monarchy.[38] (1823)

In all these formulations, the Whig and Tory parties,
which arise by nature and prevail one over the other in all
governments but the American, have become aspects, features, powers, or branches of the American government.
Clearly Jefferson takes for granted a transformation of natural parties in the people to artificial, created parts of the
government. He presupposes the existence in America for
the first time, of representative government. There was general agreement among the Framers and the political philosophers on whom they relied, that representative government
was a modern invention to make a large society capable of
governing itself freely. "The introduction of this new principle of representative democracy," Jefferson went so far as to

[36]Letter to Abigail Adams, September 11, 1804, *AJ*, vol. 1, p.
280.
[37]Letter to John Adams, June 27, 1813, *AJ*, vol. 2, p. 336.
[38]Letter to the Marquis de Lafayette, November 4, 1823, *Writings*, vol. 10, p. 282.

say, "has rendered useless almost everything written before on the structure of government . . ."[39]

Under the new principle, it was generally admitted that the purpose of government was to represent and not to impose itself on society, because men were individuals outside government before they created government to serve as an instrument to their ends. In Jefferson's conception, however, the fact that men were once unconnected individuals in the "state of nature" is not so important. What matters is that the people have always been divided and formed into natural parties of "two classes of sentiment," for representative government represents these partisan sentiments rather than individuals. Since it reflects the existence of both natural parties in its branches (which are three, not two), neither natural party can rule over the other in the manner of modern monarchies, on one hand, or of ancient democracies, on the other. Artificial, constitutional government can then be based on the natural mixture of parties in every society, and representative government in this sense, the *true* representative government, is what Jefferson calls republican.[40]

Republican government recognizes and harmonizes the opposite tendencies of government to be found in the people by nature. The natural parties do not quite constitute a natural harmony, for men still need to make government for themselves; but they constitute the natural basis for the artificial harmony that men make. The natural parties are *political* parties, be it noted; they are not economic interests but parties promoting a certain kind of rule. In addition, they have in their natural state a principle on which their artificial harmony can build, the *lex majoris partis*, "that fundamental law of nature, by which alone self-government can be exercised by a society." Jefferson believed that a people must be taught this law. Though it exists by nature, men must learn "the habit of acknowledging" it; and the American Revolution, as compared to the French, succeeded because the

[39]Letter to Isaac H. Tiffany, August 26, 1816, *The Political Writings of Thomas Jefferson*, ed. Edward Dumbauld, p. 87.
[40]Letter to Dupont de Nemours, April 24, 1816, *Writings*, vol. 10, p. 24.

American people had learned this habit so well "that with them it is almost innate."[41]

Republican *government* reflects and assures the balance of natural parties in the people, and the Republican *party* promotes republican government. But to do so, it advocates trusting the people for their capability in self-government, which is supported by the balance of natural parties to be found in the people and shown in their habit of obeying the natural law of majority rule. The people are trustworthy because, containing the two natural parties and living under the law of majority rule, they are impartial. Jefferson always said, therefore, that his party was distinguished from its opponent by its republican trust of the people, compared to the antirepublican fear of the people.

There is one party in the government and among the people, the Republican, which restores the balance of both parties, although both parties are natural and have a right to exist both in the people and as powers in the government. The apparent indifference of the Declaration of Independence to forms of government is explained and justified by the impartiality of republican government. But the republican party as the impartial party has by nature a preferred status. That is why Jefferson could admit that "the parties of Whig and Tory, are those of nature," and yet assert in the same place: "The sickly, weakly, timid man, fears the people, and is a tory by nature. The healthy, strong and bold, cherishes them, and is formed a whig by nature."[42] To be a tory is to be the victim of an incurable, congenital disease and the cause of an occasional epidemic in the people, for which the Whigs in a body are the doctor, themselves robust and not too sympathetic to the incurably sick.

When Jefferson, the republican doctor, was elected to the presidency in 1800, he thought it a marvelous event: a revolution comparable to the revolution that began in 1776, indeed a revolution that for the first time established the principles of 1776. Writing to Joseph Priestley just after his

[41]Letter to John Breckenridge, January 29, 1800, *Writings*, vol. 7, p. 417.
[42]Letter to the Marquis de Lafayette, November 4, 1823, *Writings*, vol. 10, p. 281.

inauguration, Jefferson made no effort to contain his enthusiasm. "We can no longer say there is nothing new under
the sun. For this whole chapter in the history of man is
new. . . . The mighty wave of public opinion which rolled
over [our Republic] is new. But the most pleasing novelty is,
its so quickly subsiding over such an extent of surface to its
true level again."[43] In his moment of triumph, Jefferson
proclaimed the most pleasing aspect of the triumph to be its
accomplishment with "order and good sense" and without
bloodshed. One is compelled to acknowledge the sincerity
of his statement of conciliation in his First Inaugural Address. "But every difference of opinion is not a difference of
principle. We have called, by different names, brethren of
the same principle. We are all republicans: we are all federalists." The Republican party did not claim victory because it
did not aim at a mere party triumph, as had the democrats
of old. It aimed, as Jefferson saw it, at the restoration of a
republican balance in which the republican party was but
one factor, if the preferred factor.

This ambiguity of "republican" entails the ambivalence
toward monarchy that we have seen in Jefferson's thought.
On the one hand, his party attacked the Federalists above all
for favoring monarchy and for being "monocrats"; on the
other, it allowed a limited monarchy in the office of the
president and even promoted Jefferson to that dignity. The
natural tory party has its legitimate representative in the
monarchical *power* of modern republican government, and
precisely because the tories do have this representative, they
need not fear republican government and the people who
support it. If they do fear the people nevertheless, if a natural tory such as John Adams or even George Washington
receives the office, or if an Alexander Hamilton manages it,
then the people may need to give the monarchical power to
a partisan republican.

Jefferson seems to have understood the evil of monarchy
as one aspect of a more general evil, that of "consolidated
government," also described thus: ". . . what has destroyed
liberty and the rights of man in every government which has
ever existed under the sun? The generalizing and concen-

[43]Letter to Joseph Priestley, March 21, 1801, *Writings*, vol. 8,
p. 22.

trating all cares and powers into one body, no matter
whether of the autocrats of Russia or France, or of the aristocrats of a Venetian senate."[44] When monarchy is seen as one
of the powers in republican government and the tendency
to monarchy as the wider evil of consolidating power, one
can make sense of Jefferson's seemingly exaggerated fear. It
was not that he anticipated the appearance of an exact copy
of the British or any other king in America; he was apprehen-
sive that the separation of powers would be violated. Under
Hamilton's influence, he thought, the Federalist party in the
1790s was establishing a "paper system," a nexus of bankers
and bondholders which constituted the real government behind the mask of formal republican correctness. It had found
a way to interpret and administer the Constitution for this
purpose in the British policy, founded by the Whigs of 1688
and practiced by the anti-American imperialists of the
1770s, of allying financial and political interests. The task of
the Republican party was to take off this mask and expose
the British system to the just and effectual indignation of the
people.

Jefferson's thought on states' rights arises from the same
apprehension as his thought on monarchy. As he feared a
consolidation of power in the "more permanent powers" of
the national government, so he feared the same in the national government as a whole opposed to the states. He
believed that the Federalist system that subverted the principle of separation of powers subverted the principle of feder-
alism at the same time, for the two principles have the same
function of representing the natural parties. The executive,
the Senate, the judiciary and the national government he
considered the more permanent powers; the House of Representatives and the states the more popular.[45] Thus in 1798
Jefferson authored the Kentucky resolutions declaring the

[44]Letter to William Johnson, October 17, 1822, *Writings*, vol. 10,
p. 225; letter to Joseph C. Cabell, February 2, 1816, *Political
Writings*, ed. Edward Dumbauld, p. 99. Jefferson would have
been willing to add "or of the democrats of an Athenian assembly
. . ."; Letter to A. Coray, October 31, 1823, *The Life and Selected
Writings of Thomas Jefferson*, ed. A. Koch and W. Peden, p. 111.
[45]Letter to the Marquis de Lafayette, November 4, 1823, *Writings*, vol. 10, p. 282.

Alien and Sedition Acts passed by the Federalist Congress null and void. These acts were aimed at subversion from partisans of the French revolution; they struck the nerve of Jefferson's party, since he expected them to be used against the republican newspapers and editors (some of whom were aliens).

In the Kentucky resolutions, he propounded the theory that the Constitution was a compact of the states, and the "General Government" thus a creature with delegated powers of whose extent the states would have to be the final judge. Without commenting on the accuracy or the later history of this celebrated doctrine, one may remark that it reflects Jefferson's own understanding of representative government.

"Representation" is a method whereby the people are governed by their own choice, but theorists and statesmen who accept this method can differ on how the people should express their choice. Whereas most thought that government could be effective only at a certain distance from the people, so that the people could not lightly or easily change their minds, Jefferson had greater confidence that the people, obeying the natural law of majority rule, could change their minds without turbulence and bloodshed. He thought he saw an example of profound but peaceable revolution in his own election in 1800. The basis of his confidence, however, was the virtue of the independent farmer. If that basis no longer exists, or never existed, some substitute must be found and his theory rethought.

Jefferson became the founder, or one of the founders, of party government in America (in the contemporary sense), despite his intention. Although he believed that men are naturally divided into two parties, he never intended a public coexistence, permanent establishment and occasional alternation of the two parties. For him, republican balance served the purpose of party government in this sense, and the party was a temporary and emergency instrument of the people to correct the abuses of government and to tame the monarchical powers. Thus, though "monarchy" had its necessary place in the government, the only legitimate party was the Republican party, because it was the only party that the people could use. He never ceased to hope that his Republican party, by conciliating its opponents, could safely disappear. We may smile at Jefferson's naïveté, but he would be dismayed to see that American political parties, having become semiofficial institutions, now seem as remote from the people as the government they were designed to correct and purge. He once exclaimed: "If I could not go to heaven but with a party, I would not go there at all."[46] This makes it clear that his disgust for partisanship exceeds his attraction to heaven, but it does not say whether he thought a party necessary to deal with human corruption. He did think so, and he also thought it necessary, for the public good as well as for partisan success, to keep the Republican party temporary by deploring partisanship and by concealing his own partisanship. He once said to a friend on a partisan matter: "Do not let my name be connected with the business"[47]—which could serve as the motto of the modern partisan at work.

The necessity of partisanship diminishes the dignity of politics. This need not be so, it would seem, for a statesman who advances a cause; and Jefferson surely had a cause and advanced it. But his cause was not his own; it was the people's cause. He could appear only as the servant or at best the champion of men who, though in his view honest and industrious, were less remarkable than he. Their cause could never fully be his, since they could share only as beneficiaries and not as participants in the life of science and in the most difficult tasks of politics, such as the making of constitutions and the progress of reform. Jefferson was bound to feel a tension between his sense of his own powers and his understanding of his duty to the people. When shocked and disappointed at unfair criticism of his tenure as governor of Virginia, he could wonder whether the state can command the service of its members to an indefinite extent. "If we are made in some degree for others, yet in a greater we are made for ourselves."[48]

He also said, to the contrary, that "the essence of virtue

---

[46]Letter to Francis Hopkinson, March 13, 1789, *Writings*, vol. 5, p. 76.
[47]Quoted in Noble E. Cunningham, Jr., *The Jeffersonian Republicans*, p. 131.
[48]*Papers*, vol. 6, p. 185.

is in doing good to others. . . ." But what is good to others must be decided by utility: ". . . Nature has constituted *utility* to man, the standard and test of virtue."[49] Virtue cannot be precious in itself if it is not precious above all for oneself. In politics, Jefferson devoted his partisanship to an ideal of nonpartisanship, an independent, republican people. Where was his place in this people? His political thought as we have explained it centers on the unity of independence and virtue in a people, but he did not provide for the same unity for "natural aristocrats" like himself. In his hands the truth of equality was too abstract; there was not enough justice for himself. His partisanship was based on the self-forgetting of the modern idealist, whose cause is not the public good but always someone else's good. In Jefferson's case, the failure to include himself in republican principles led to overconfidence in the system of republican balance. The problems of equality Jefferson had so well identified, especially the problem of slavery, were lost to sight as men put their faith in Jefferson's institutional solution; for many of the Jeffersonians came to think that slavery had a place in the republican balance itself.

[49] Letter to John Adams, October 14, 1816, *AJ*, vol. 2, p. 492; Letter to Thomas Law, June 13, 1814, *Life and Selected Writings*, ed. A. Koch and W. Peden, p. 639.

principal dates in the life of Thomas Jefferson

April 13, 1743	Born at Shadwell, Virginia, son of Peter Jefferson, a surveyor.
1760–1762	Attended William and Mary College.
1767	Admitted to the Bar.
1769	Elected to the Virginia House of Burgesses.
1772	Married to Martha Wayles Skelton.
1774	Elected to Virginia's first revolutionary assembly.
1775	Accepted a Virginia seat in the Second Continental Congress at Philadelphia.
June 11, 1776	Appointed head of a committee to draw up a declaration of independence.
July 4, 1776	Jefferson's draft of the Declaration of Independence adopted with minor revisions.
1776	Returned to Virginia, began a comprehensive project for the "Revisal" of Virginia's laws.
1777	Drafted bill establishing religious freedom.
June 1, 1779	Elected Governor of Virginia
1781–1782	Writing *Notes on the State of Virginia.*
1783	Member of Congress under the Articles of Confederation.
1785	Minister to France.
1790–1793	Secretary of State.
1796	Elected Vice-President.
1798	Secretly drafted the Kentucky Resolutions against the Alien and Sedition Acts.
1801–1809	Served as third President of the United States.
1803	Signed a treaty for the Louisiana Purchase.
1807	Signed the Embargo Act.

1819   University of Virginia chartered; built un-
                der Jefferson's direction, its Faculty was
                selected and its curriculum formed by
                him.

July 4, 1826   Died at Monticello on the fiftieth anniver-
                sary of the Declaration of Indepen-
                dence.

A Summary View of the Rights of British America[1]

Resolved, that it be an instruction to the said deputies, when assembled in General Congress, with the deputies from the other states of British America, to propose to the said Congress, that an humble and dutiful address be presented to his Majesty, begging leave to lay before him, as Chief Magistrate of the British empire, the united complaints of his Majesty's subjects in America; complaints which are excited by many unwarrantable encroachments and usurpations, attempted to be made by the legislature of one part of the empire, upon the rights which God, and the laws, have given equally and independently to all. To represent to his Majesty that these, his States, have often individually made humble application to his imperial Throne, to obtain, through its intervention, some redress of their injured rights; to none of which, was ever even an answer condescended. Humbly to hope that this, their joint address, penned in the language of truth, and divested of those expressions of servility, which would persuade his Majesty that we are asking favors, and not rights, shall obtain from his Majesty a more respectful acceptance; and this his Majesty will think we have reason to expect, when he reflects that he is no more than the chief officer of the people, appointed by the laws, and circumscribed with definite powers, to assist in working the great machine of government, erected for their use, and, consequently, subject to their superintendence; and, in order that these, our rights, as well as the invasions of them, may be laid more fully before his Majesty, to take a view of them, from the origin and first settlement of these countries.

[1]This pamphlet, which may be considered a prelude to the Declaration of Independence, was published in Williamsburg, Virginia in 1774, then reprinted in Philadelphia and London.—*Editor*

To remind him that our ancestors, before their emigration to America, were the free inhabitants of the British dominions in Europe, and possessed a right, which nature has given to all men, of departing from the country in which chance, not choice, has placed them, of going in quest of new habitations, and of there establishing new societies, under such laws and regulations as, to them, shall seem most likely to promote public happiness. . . .

We do not, however, mean to underrate those aids, which, to us, were doubtless valuable, on whatever principles granted: but we would shew that they cannot give a title to that authority which the British Parliament would arrogate over us; and that may amply be repaid by our giving to the inhabitants of Great Britain such exclusive privileges in trade as may be advantageous to them, and, at the same time, not too restrictive to ourselves. That settlement having been thus effected in the wilds of America, the emigrants thought proper to adopt that system of laws, under which they had hitherto lived in the mother country, and to continue their union with her, by submitting themselves to the same common sovereign, who was thereby made the central link, connecting the several parts of the empire thus newly multiplied. . . .

That thus have we hastened through the reigns which preceded his Majesty's, during which the violation of our rights were less alarming, because repeated at more distant intervals, than that rapid and bold succession of injuries, which is likely to distinguish the present from all other periods of American story. Scarcely have our minds been able to emerge from the astonishment into which one stroke of Parliamentary thunder has involved us, before another more heavy and more alarming is fallen on us. Single acts of tyranny may be ascribed to the accidental opinion of a day; but a series of oppressions, begun at a distinguished period, and pursued unalterably through every change of ministers, too plainly prove a deliberate, systematical plan of reducing us to slavery. . . .

That one other act, passed in the same 7th year of the reign, having been a peculiar attempt, must ever require peculiar mention; it is entitled "An act for suspending the legislature of New York."

One free and independent legislature, hereby takes upon itself to suspend the powers of another, free and indepen-

dent as itself. Thus exhibiting a phenomenon unknown in
nature, the creator, and creature of its own power. Not only
the principles of common sense, but the common feelings of
human nature must be surrendered up, before his Majesty's
subjects here, can be persuaded to believe, that they hold
their political existence at the will of a British Parliament.
Shall these governments be dissolved, their property an-
nihilated, and their people reduced to a state of nature, at
the imperious breath of a body of men whom they never saw,
in whom they never confided, and over whom they have no
powers of punishment or removal, let their crimes against
the American public be ever so great? Can any one reason
be assigned, why one hundred and sixty thousand electors
in the island of Great Britain, should give law to four millions in the States of America, every individual of whom is
equal to every individual of them in virtue, in understanding, and in bodily strength? Were this to be admitted,
instead of being a free people, as we have hitherto supposed,
and mean to continue ourselves, we should suddenly be
found the slaves, not of one, but of one hundred and sixty
thousand tyrants; distinguished, too, from all others, by this
singular circumstance, that they are removed from the reach
of fear, the only restraining motive which may hold the hand
of a tyrant. . . .

That these are the acts of power, assumed by a body of
men foreign to our constitutions, and unacknowledged by
our laws; against which we do, on behalf of the inhabitants
of British America, enter this, our solemn and determined
protest. And we do earnestly intreat his Majesty, as yet the
only mediatory power between the several States of the British empire, to recommend to his Parliament of Great Britain, the total revocation of these acts, which, however
nugatory they may be, may yet prove the cause of further
discontents and jealousies among us.

That we next proceed to consider the conduct of his
Majesty, as holding the Executive powers of the laws of these
States, and mark out his deviations from the line of duty. By
the Constitution of Great Britain, as well as of the several
American States, his Majesty possesses the power of refusing to pass into a law, any bill which has already passed the
other two branches of the legislature. His Majesty, however,
and his ancestors, conscious of the impropriety of opposing
their single opinion to the united wisdom of two Houses of

Parliament, while their proceedings were unbiassed by interested principles, for several ages past, have modestly declined the exercise of this power, in that part of his empire called Great Britain. But, by change of circumstances, other principles than those of justice simply, have obtained an influence on their determinations. The addition of new States to the British empire has produced an addition of new, and, sometimes, opposite interests. It is now, therefore, the great office of his Majesty to resume the exercise of his negative power, and to prevent the passage of laws by any one legislature of the empire, which might bear injuriously on the rights and interests of another. Yet this will not excuse the wanton exercise of this power, which we have seen his Majesty practice on the laws of the American legislature. For the most trifling reasons, and, sometimes for no conceivable reason at all, his Majesty has rejected laws of the most salutary tendency. The abolition of domestic slavery is the great object of desire in those colonies, where it was, unhappily, introduced in their infant state. But previous to the enfranchisement of the slaves we have, it is necessary to exclude all further importations from Africa. Yet our repeated attempts to effect this, by prohibitions, and by imposing duties which might amount to a prohibition, having been hitherto defeated by his Majesty's negative: thus preferring the immediate advantages of a few British corsairs, to the lasting interests of the American States, and to the rights of human nature, deeply wounded by this infamous practice. Nay, the single interposition of an interested individual against a law was scarcely ever known to fail of success, though, in the opposite scale, were placed the interests of a whole country. That this is so shameful an abuse of a power, trusted with his Majesty for other purposes, as if, not reformed, would call for some legal restrictions. . . .

When the representative body have lost the confidence of their constituents, when they have notoriously made sale of their most valuable rights, when they have assumed to themselves powers which the people never put into their hands, then, indeed, their continuing in office becomes dangerous to the State, and calls for an exercise of the power of dissolution. Such being the cause for which the representative body should, and should not, be dissolved, will it not appear strange, to an unbiassed observer, that that of Great Britain was not dissolved, while those of the colonies have repeatedly incurred that sentence?

But your Majesty, or your Governors, have carried this power beyond every limit known or provided for by the laws. After dissolving one House of Representatives, they have refused to call another, so that, for a great length of time, the legislature provided by the laws, has been out of existence. From the nature of things, every society must, at all times, possess within itself the sovereign powers of legislation. The feelings of human nature revolt against the supposition of a State so situated, as that it may not, in any emergency, provide against dangers which, perhaps, threaten immediate ruin. While those bodies are in existence to whom the people have delegated the powers of legislation, they alone possess, and may exercise, those powers. But when they are dissolved, by the lopping off one or more of their branches, the power reverts to the people, who may use it to unlimited extent, either assembling together in person, sending deputies, or in any other way they may think proper. We forbear to trace consequences further; the dangers are conspicuous with which this practice is replete. . . .

That, in order to enforce the arbitrary measures before complained of, his Majesty has, from time to time, sent among us large bodies of armed forces, not made up of the people here, nor raised by the authority of our laws. Did his Majesty possess such a right as this, it might swallow up all our other rights, whenever he should think proper. But his Majesty has no right to land a single armed man on our shores; and those whom he sends here are liable to our laws, for the suppression and punishment of riots, routs, and unlawful assemblies, or are hostile bodies invading us in defiance of law. When, in the course of the late war, it became expedient that a body of Hanoverian troops should be brought over for the defence of Great Britain, his Majesty's grandfather, our late sovereign, did not pretend to introduce them under any authority he possessed. Such a measure would have given just alarm to his subjects of Great Britain, whose liberties would not be safe if armed men of another country, and of another spirit, might be brought into the realm at any time, without the consent of their legislature. He, therefore, applied to Parliament, who passed an act for that purpose, limiting the number to be brought in, and the time they were to continue. In like manner is his Majesty restrained in every part of the empire. He possesses indeed the executive power of the laws in every State; but they are the laws of the particular State, which he is to administer within that State, and not those of any one within the limits of another. Every State must judge for itself, the number of armed men which they may safely trust among them, of whom they are to consist, and under what restrictions they are to be laid. To render these proceedings still more criminal against our laws, instead of subjecting the military to the civil power, his majesty has expressly made the civil subordinate to the military. But can his Majesty thus put down all law under his feet? Can he erect a power superior to that which erected himself? He has done it indeed by force; but let him remember that force cannot give right.

That these are our grievances, which we have thus laid before his Majesty, with that freedom of language and sentiment which becomes a free people claiming their rights as derived from the laws of nature, and not as the gift of their Chief Magistrate. Let those flatter, who fear: it is not an American art. To give praise where it is not due might be well from the venal, but would ill beseem those who are asserting the rights of human nature. They know, and will, therefore, say, that Kings are the servants, not the proprietors of the people. Open your breast, Sire, to liberal and expanded thought. Let not the name of George the Third, be a blot on the page of history. You are surrounded by British counsellors, but remember that they are parties. You have no ministers for American affairs, because you have none taken from among us, nor amenable to the laws on which they are to give you advice. It behooves you, therefore, to think and to act for yourself and your people. The great principles of right and wrong are legible to every reader; to pursue them, requires not the aid of many counsellors. The whole art of government consists in the art of being honest. Only aim to do your duty, and mankind will give you credit where you fail. No longer persevere in sacrificing the rights of one part of the empire to the inordinate desires of another; but deal out to all, equal and impartial right. Let no act be passed by any one legislature, which may infringe on the rights and liberties of another. This is the important post in which fortune has placed you, holding the balance of a great, if a well-poised empire. This, Sire, is

the advice of your great American council, on the obser-
vance of which may perhaps depend your felicity and future
fame, and the preservation of that harmony which alone can
continue, both to Great Britain and America, the reciprocal
advantages of their connection. It is neither our wish nor our
interest to separate from her. We are willing, on our part,
to sacrifice everything which reason can ask, to the restoration of that tranquillity for which all must wish. On their
part, let them be ready to establish union on a generous
plan. Let them name their terms, but let them be just. Accept
of every commercial preference it is in our power to give, for
such things as we can raise for their use, or they make for
ours. But let them not think to exclude us from going to
other markets to dispose of those commodities which they
cannot use, nor to supply those wants which they cannot
supply. Still less, let it be proposed, that our properties,
within our own territories, shall be taxed or regulated by any
power on earth, but our own. The God who gave us life,
gave us liberty at the same time: the hand of force may
destroy, but cannot disjoin them. This, Sire, is our last, our
determined resolution. And that you will be pleased to inter-
pose, with that efficacy which your earnest endeavors may
insure, to procure redress of these our great grievances, to
quiet the minds of your subjects in British America against
any apprehensions of future encroachment, to establish fra-
ternal love and harmony through the whole empire, and that
that may continue to the latest ages of time, is the fervent
prayer of all British America.

The Declaration of Independence

JULY 4, 1776

When in the course of human events it becomes necessary
for one people to dissolve the political bands which have
connected them with another, and to assume among the
powers of the earth, the separate and equal station to which

the Laws of Nature and of Nature's God entitle them, a decent respect to the opinions of mankind requires that they should declare the causes which impel them to the separation.

We hold these truths to be self-evident, that all men are created equal, that they are endowed by their Creator with certain unalienable Rights, that among these are Life, Liberty and the pursuit of Happiness.—That to secure these rights, Governments are instituted among Men, deriving their just powers from the consent of the governed.—That whenever any Form of Government becomes destructive of these ends, it is the Right of the People to alter or to abolish it, and to institute new Government, laying its foundation on such principles, and organizing its powers in such form, as to them shall seem most likely to effect their Safety and Happiness. Prudence, indeed, will dictate that Governments long established should not be changed for light and transient causes; and accordingly all experience hath shewn, that mankind are more disposed to suffer, while evils are sufferable, than to right themselves by abolishing the forms to which they are accustomed. But when a long train of abuses and usurpations, pursuing invariably the same Object, evinces a design to reduce them under absolute Despotism, it is their right, it is their duty, to throw off such Government, and to provide new Guards for their future security. —Such has been the patient sufferance of these Colonies; and such is now the necessity which constrains them to alter their former Systems of Government. The history of the present King of Great Britain is a history of repeated injuries and usurpations, all having in direct object the establishment of an absolute Tyranny over these States. To prove this, let Facts be submitted to a candid world.

He has refused his Assent to Laws, the most wholesome and necessary for the public good.

He has forbidden his Governors to pass Laws of immediate and pressing importance, unless suspended in their operation till his Assent should be obtained; and when so suspended, he has utterly neglected to attend to them.

He has refused to pass other Laws for the accommodation of large districts of people, unless those people would relinquish the right of Representation in the Legislature, a right inestimable to them and formidable to tyrants only.

He has called together legislative bodies at places unusual, uncomfortable, and distant from the depository of their public Records, for the sole purpose of fatiguing them into compliance with his measures.

He has dissolved Representative Houses repeatedly, for opposing with manly firmness his invasions on the rights of the people.

He has refused for a long time, after such dissolutions, to cause others to be elected; whereby the Legislative powers, incapable of Annihilation, have returned to the People at large for their exercise; the State remaining in the mean time exposed to all the dangers of invasion from without, and convulsions within.

He has endeavoured to prevent the population of these States; for that purpose obstructing the Laws for Naturalization of Foreigners; refusing to pass others to encourage their migrations hither, and raising the conditions of new Appropriations of Lands.

He has obstructed the Administration of Justice, by refusing his Assent to Laws for establishing Judiciary powers.

He has made Judges dependent on his Will alone, for the tenure of their offices, and the amount of payment of their salaries.

He has erected a multitude of New Offices, and sent hither swarms of Officers to harrass our people, and eat out their substance.

He has kept among us, in times of peace, Standing Armies without the Consent of our legislatures.

He has affected to render the Military independent of and superior to the Civil power.

He has combined with others to subject us to a jurisdiction foreign to our constitution, and unacknowledged by our laws; giving his Assent to their Acts of pretended Legislation:

For quartering large bodies of armed troops among us:

For protecting them, by a mock Trial, from punishment for any Murders which they should commit on the Inhabitants of these States:

For cutting off our Trade with all parts of the world:

For imposing Taxes on us without our Consent:

For depriving us in many cases, of the benefits of Trial by Jury:

For transporting us beyond Seas to be tried for pretended offences:

For abolishing the free System of English Laws in a neighbouring Province, establishing therein an Arbitrary government, and enlarging its Boundaries so as to render it at once an example and fit instrument for introducing the same absolute rule into these Colonies:

For taking away our Charters, abolishing our most valuable Laws, and altering fundamentally the Forms of our Governments:

For suspending our own Legislatures, and declaring themselves invested with power to legislate for us in all cases whatsoever.

He has abdicated Government here, by declaring us out of his Protection and waging War against us.

He has plundered our seas, ravaged our Coasts, burnt our towns, and destroyed the lives of our people.

He is at this time transporting large Armies of foreign Mercenaries to compleat the works of death, desolation and tyranny, already begun with circumstances of Cruelty & perfidy scarcely paralleled in the most barbarous ages, and totally unworthy the Head of a civilized nation.

He has constrained our fellow Citizens taken Captive on the high Seas to bear Arms against their Country, to become the executioners of their friends and Brethren, or to fall themselves by their Hands.

He has excited domestic insurrections amongst us, and has endeavoured to bring on the inhabitants of our frontiers; the merciless Indian Savages, whose known rule of warfare, is an undistinguished destruction of all ages, sexes and conditions.

In every stage of these Oppressions We have Petitioned for Redress in the most humble terms: Our repeated Petitions have been answered only by repeated injury. A Prince, whose character is thus marked by every act which may define a Tyrant, is unfit to be the ruler of a free people.

Nor have We been wanting in attentions to our British brethren. We have warned them from time to time of attempts by their legislature to extend an unwarrantable jurisdiction over us. We have reminded them of the circumstances of our emigration and settlement here. We have appealed to their native justice and magnanimity, and we have conjured them by the ties of our common kindred to disavow these usurpations, which would inevitably interrupt our connections and correspondence. They too have been deaf to the voice of justice and of consanguinity. We must, therefore, acquiesce in the necessity, which denounces our Separation, and hold them, as we hold the rest of mankind, Enemies in War, in Peace Friends.

We, therefore, the Representatives of the united States of America, in General Congress, Assembled, appealing to the Supreme Judge of the world for the rectitude of our intentions, do, in the Name, and by Authority of the good People of these Colonies solemnly publish and declare, That these United Colonies are, and of Right ought to be Free and Independent States; that they are Absolved from all Allegiance to the British Crown, and that all political connection between them and the State of Great Britain, is and ought to be totally dissolved; and that as Free and Independent States, they have full Power to levy War, conclude Peace, contract Alliances, establish Commerce, and to do all other Acts and Things which Independent States may of right do.

And for the support of this Declaration, with a firm reliance on the protection of divine Providence, we mutually pledge to each other our Lives, our Fortunes and our sacred Honor.

Two Letters on the Declaration

To Henry Lee, May 8, 1825

But with respect to our rights, and the acts of the British government contravening those rights, there was but one opinion on this side of the water. All American Whigs thought alike on these subjects. When forced, therefore, to resort to arms for redress, an appeal to the tribunal of the world was deemed proper for our justification. This was the object of the Declaration of Independence. Not to find out new principles, or new arguments, never before thought of, not merely to say things which had never been said before;

but to place before mankind the common sense of the subject, in terms so plain and firm as to command their assent, and to justify ourselves in the independent stand we are compelled to take. Neither aiming at originality of principle or sentiment, nor yet copied from any particular and previous writing, it was intended to be an expression of the American mind, and to give to that expression the proper tone and spirit called for by the occasion. All its authority rests then on the harmonizing sentiments of the day, whether expressed in conversation, in letters, printed essays, or in the elementary books of public right, as Aristotle, Cicero, Locke, Sidney, etc. The historical documents which you mention as in your possession, ought all to be found, and I am persuaded you will find, to be corroborative of the facts and principles advanced in that Declaration. . . .

To Roger C. Weightman, June 24, 1826

The kind invitation I receive from you, on the part of the citizens of the city of Washington, to be present with them at their celebration on the fiftieth anniversary of American Independence, as one of the surviving signers of an instrument pregnant with our own, and the fate of the world, is most flattering to myself, and heightened by the honorable accompaniment proposed for the comfort of such a journey. It adds sensibly to the sufferings of sickness, to be deprived by it of a personal participation in the rejoicings of that day. But acquiescence is a duty, under circumstances not placed among those we are permitted to control. I should, indeed, with peculiar delight, have met and exchanged there congratulations personally with the small band, the remnant of that host of worthies, who joined with us on that day, in the bold and doubtful election we were to make for our country, between submission or the sword; and to have enjoyed with them the consolatory fact, that our fellow citizens, after half a century of experience and prosperity, continue to approve the choice we made. May it be to the world, what I believe it will be (to some parts sooner, to others later, but finally to all), the signal of arousing men to burst the chains under which monkish ignorance and superstition had persuaded them to bind themselves, and to assume the blessings and security of self-government. That form which we have su stituted, restores the free right to the unbounded exercis of reason and freedom of opinion. All eyes are opened, o opening, to the rights of man. The general spread of the light of science has already laid open to every view the palpable truth, that the mass of mankind has not been born with saddles on their backs, nor a favored few booted and spurred, ready to ride them legitimately, by the grace of God. These are grounds of hope for others. For ourselves, let the annual return of this day forever refresh our recollections of these rights, and an undiminished devotion to them. . . .

An Act for Establishing Religious Freedom[1]

Well aware that Almighty God hath created the mind free; that all attempts to influence it by temporal punishments or burdens, or by civil incapacitations, tend only to beget habits of hypocrisy and meanness, and are a departure from the plan of the Holy Author of our religion, who being Lord both of body and mind, yet chose not to propagate it by coercions on either, as was in his Almighty power to do; that the impious presumption of legislators and rulers, civil as well as ecclesiastical, who, being themselves but fallible and uninspired men have assumed dominion over the faith of others, setting up their own opinions and modes of thinking as the only true and infallible, and as such endeavoring to impose them on others, hath established and maintained

[1]This Virginia statute was drafted by Jefferson in 1777, debated in the Virginia House of Delegates in 1779, brought forward again by James Madison in 1785 and adopted in 1786. The text is printed in the 1784 *Report of the Committee of Revisors* and was regarded by Jefferson as one of his best statements on a matter he considered vital to the principles of the Declaration. He asked that his authorship of it be one of the three items recorded on his tombstone.—*Editor*

very general; does not back up

...se religions over the greatest part of the world, and
through all time; that to compel a man to furnish contributions of money for the propagation of opinions which he
disbelieves, is sinful and tyrannical; that even the forcing
him to support this or that teacher of his own religious
persuasion, is depriving him of the comfortable liberty of
giving his contributions to the particular pastor whose morals he would make his pattern, and whose powers he feels
most persuasive to righteousness, and is withdrawing from
the ministry those temporal rewards, which proceeding
from an approbation of their personal conduct, are an addi-
tional incitement to earnest and unremitting labors for the
instruction of mankind; that our civil rights have no dependence on our religious opinions, more than our opinions in
physics or geometry; that, therefore, the proscribing any
citizen as unworthy the public confidence by laying upon
him an incapacity of being called to the offices of trust and
emolument, unless he profess or renounce this or that religious opinion, is depriving him injuriously of those privileges and advantages to which in common with his fellow
citizens he has a natural right; that it tends also to corrupt
the principles of that very religion it is meant to encourage,
by bribing, with a monopoly of wordly honors and emolu-
ments, those who will externally profess and conform to it;
that though indeed these are criminal who do not withstand
such temptation, yet neither are those innocent who lay the
bait in their way; that to suffer the civil magistrate to intrude
his powers into the field of opinion and to restrain the pro-
fession or propagation of principles, on the supposition of
their ill tendency, is a dangerous fallacy, which at once destroys all religious liberty, because he being of course judge
of that tendency, will make his opinions the rule of judgment, and approve or condemn the sentiments of others
only as they shall square with or differ from his own; that it
is time enough for the rightful purposes of civil government,
for its offices to interfere when principles break out into
overt acts against peace and good order; and finally, that
truth is great and will prevail if left to herself, that she is the
proper and sufficient antagonist to error, and has nothing to
fear from the conflict, unless by human interposition dis-
armed of her natural weapons, free argument and debate,
errors ceasing to be dangerous when it is permitted freely
to contradict them.

Be it therefore enacted by the General Assembly, That no man shall be compelled to frequent or support any religious worship, place or ministry whatsoever, nor shall be enforced, restrained, molested, or burthened in his body or goods, nor shall otherwise suffer on account of his religious opinions of belief; but that all men shall be free to profess, and by argument to maintain, their opinions in matters of religion, and that the same shall in nowise diminish, enlarge, or affect their civil capacities.

And though we well know this Assembly, elected by the people for the ordinary purposes of legislation only, have no power to restrain the acts of succeeding assemblies, constituted with the powers equal to our own, and that therefore to declare this act irrevocable, would be of no effect in law, yet we are free to declare, and do declare, that the rights hereby asserted are of the natural rights of mankind, and that if any act shall be hereafter passed to repeal the present or to narrow its operation, such act will be an infringement of natural right.

Notes on the State of Virginia[1]

Query VI: Productions Mineral, Vegetable and Animal

Near the eastern foot of the North mountain are immense bodies of *Schist,* containing impressions of shells in a variety of forms. I have received petrified shells of very different kinds from the first sources of the Kentucky, which bear no resemblance to any I have ever seen on the tide-waters. It

[1]In an "Advertisement" preceding this work, Jefferson said that he wrote the *Notes* in 1781 and 1782 in answer to queries proposed to him by a "foreigner of distinction," the Abbé de Marbois. Its chapters are therefore presented as "Queries" with Jefferson's answers. In Query VI we pick up Jefferson's geographical description as he stops to comment on "an universal deluge," that is, on the likelihood of the Biblical flood. He ends with a statement recommending skepticism in case of doubt. In these excerpts, almost all of Jefferson's notes have been omitted.—*Editor*

is said that shells are found in the Andes, in South America, fifteen thousand feet above the level of the ocean. This is considered by many, both of the learned and unlearned, as a proof of an universal deluge. To the many considerations opposing this opinion, the following may be added. The atmosphere, and all its contents, whether of water, air, or other matters, gravitate to the earth; that is to say, they have weight. Experience tells us, that the weight of all these together never exceeds that of a column of mercury of 31 inches height, which is equal to one of rainwater of 35 feet high. If the whole contents of the atmosphere then were water, instead of what they are, it would cover the globe but 35 feet deep; but as these waters, as they fell, would run into the seas, the superficial measure of which is to that of the dry parts of the globe as two to one, the seas would be raised only 52½ feet above their present level, and of course would overflow the lands to that height only. In Virginia this would be a very small proportion even of the champaign country, the banks of our tide-waters being frequently, if not generally, of a greater height. Deluges beyond this extent then, as for instance, to the North mountain or to Kentucky, seem out of the laws of nature. But within it they may have taken place to a greater or less degree, in proportion to the combination of natural causes which may be supposed to have produced them. History renders probable some instances of a partial deluge in the country lying round the Mediterranean sea. It has been often supposed, and is not unlikely, that that sea was once a lake. While such, let us admit an extraordinary collection of the waters of the atmosphere from the other parts of the globe to have been discharged over that and the countries whose waters run into it. Or without supposing it a lake, admit such an extraordinary collection of the waters of the atmosphere, and an influx of waters from the Atlantic ocean, forced by long continued Western winds. That lake, or that sea, may thus have been so raised as to overflow the low lands adjacent to it, as those of Egypt and Armenia, which, according to a tradition of the Egyptians and Hebrews, were overflowed about 2300 years before the Christian era; those of Attica, said to have been overflowed in the time of Ogyges, about 500 years later; and those of Thessaly, in the time of Deucalion, still 300 years posterior. But such deluges as these will not account for the shells found in the higher lands. A second opinion has been entertained, which is, that, in times anterior to the records either of history or tradition, the bed of the ocean, the principal residence of the shelled tribe, has, by some great convulsion of nature, been heaved to the heights at which we now find shells and other remains of marine animals. The favourers of this opinion do well to suppose the great events on which it rests to have taken place beyond all the eras of history; for within these, certainly none such are to be found: and we may venture to say further, that no fact has taken place, either in our own days, or in the thousands of years recorded in history, which proves the existence of any natural agents, within or without the bowels of the earth, of force sufficient to heave, to the height of 15,000 feet, such masses as the Andes. The difference between the power necessary to produce such an effect, and that which shuffled together the different parts of Calabria in our days, is so immense, that, from the existence of the latter we are not authorised to infer that of the former.

M. de Voltaire has suggested a third solution of this difficulty.[2] He cites an instance in Touraine, where, in the space of 80 years, a particular spot of earth had been twice metamorphosed into soft stone, which had become hard when employed in building. In this stone shells of various kinds were produced, discoverable at first only with the microscope, but afterwards growing with the stone. From this fact, I suppose, he would have us infer, that, besides the usual process for generating shells by the elaboration of earth and water in animal vessels, nature may have provided an equivalent operation, by passing the same materials through the pores of calcareous earths and stones: as we see calcareous dropstones generating every day by the percolation of water through lime-stone, and new marble forming in the quarries from which the old has been taken out; and it might be asked, whether it is more difficult for nature to shoot the calcareous juice into the form of a shell, than other juices into the forms of chrystals, plants, animals, according to the construction of the vessels through which they pass? There

[2]Jefferson refers to "coquilles" in Voltaire's *Questions sur l' Encyclopédie,* 58 vols. Paris, 1775–1785, vol. 39, p. 147. See William Peden, ed., *Notes on the State of Virginia,* pp. 265–6.—*Editor*

is a wonder somewhere. Is it greatest on this branch of the dilemma; on that which supposes the existence of a power, of which we have no evidence in any other case; or on the first, which requires us to believe the creation of a body of water, and its subsequent annihilation? The establishment of the instance, cited by M. de Voltaire, of the growth of shells unattached to animal bodies, would have been that of his theory. But he has not established it. He has not even left it on ground so respectable as to have rendered it an object of enquiry to the literati of his own country. Abandoning this fact, therefore, the three hypotheses are equally unsatisfactory; and we must be contented to acknowledge, that this great phenomenon is as yet unsolved. Ignorance is preferable to error; and he is less remote from the truth who believes nothing, than he who believes what is wrong. . . .

Hitherto I have considered this hypothesis[3] as applied to brute animals only, and not in its extension to the man of America, whether aboriginal or transplanted. It is the opinion of Mons. de Buffon that the former furnishes no exception to it: "Although the savage of the new world is about the same height as man in our world, this does not suffice for him to constitute an exception to the general fact that all living nature has become smaller on that continent. The savage is feeble, and has small organs of generation; he has neither hair nor beard, and no ardor whatever for his female; although swifter than the European because he is better accustomed to running, he is, on the other hand, less strong in body; he is also less sensitive, and yet more timid and cowardly; he has no vivacity, no activity of mind; the activity of his body is less an exercise, a voluntary motion, than a necessary action caused by want; relieve him of hunger and thirst, and you deprive him of the active principle of all his movements; he will rest stupidly upon his legs or lying down entire days. There is no need for seeking further the cause of the isolated mode of life of these savages and their repugnance for society: the most precious spark of the fire of nature has been refused to them; they lack ardor for their females, and consequently have no love for their fellow men:

[3]The hypothesis of Buffon, the French natural scientist (1707–1788), who supposed that animals of the New World are smaller and less advanced than those of the Old World.—*Editor*

not knowing this strongest and most tender of all affections, their other feelings are also cold and languid; they love their parents and children but little; the most intimate of all ties, the family connection, binds them therefore but loosely together; between family and family there is no tie at all; hence they have no communion, no commonwealth, no state of society. Physical love constitutes their only morality; their heart is icy, their society cold, and their rule harsh. They look upon their wives only as servants for all work, or as beasts of burden, which they load without consideration with the burden of their hunting, and which they compel without mercy, without gratitude, to perform tasks which are often beyond their strength. They have only few children, and they take little care of them. Everywhere the original defect appears: they are indifferent because they have little sexual capacity, and this indifference to the other sex is the fundamental defect which weakens their nature, prevents its development, and—destroying the very germs of life—uproots society at the same time. Man is here no exception to the general rule. Nature, by refusing him the power of love, has treated him worse and lowered him deeper than any animal."[4] An afflicting picture indeed, which, for the honor of human nature, I am glad to believe has no original. Of the Indian of South America I know nothing; for I would not honor with the appelation of knowledge, what I derive from the fables published of them. These I believe to be just as true as the fables of Aesop. This belief is founded on what I have seen of man, white, red, and black, and what has been written of him by authors, enlightened themselves, and writing amidst an enlightened people. The Indian of North America being more within our reach, I can speak of him somewhat from my own knowledge, but more from the information of others better acquainted with him, and on whose truth and judgment I can rely. From these sources I am able to say, in contradiction to this representation, that he is neither more defective in ardor, nor more impotent with his female, than the white reduced to the same diet and exercise: that he is brave, when an enterprize depends on bravery; education with him making the point of honor con-

[4]Buffon, *Histoire Naturelle, Générale et Particulière,* 44 vols. Paris, 1749–1804, vol. 18, p. 146.

sist in the destruction of an enemy by stratagem, and in the
preservation of his own person free from injury; or perhaps
this is nature; while it is education which teaches us to honor
force more than finesse; that he will defend himself against
an host of enemies, always chusing to be killed, rather than
to surrender, though it be to the whites, who he knows will
treat him well: that in other situations also he meets death
with more deliberation, and endures tortures with a firmness
unknown almost to religious enthusiasm with us: that he is
affectionate to his children, careful of them, and indulgent
in the extreme: that his affections comprehend his other
connections, weakening, as with us, from circle to circle, as
they recede from the center: that his friendships are strong
and faithful to the uttermost extremity: that his sensibility is
keen, even the wariors weeping most bitterly on the loss of
their children, though in general they endeavour to appear
superior to human events: that his vivacity and activity of
mind is equal to ours in the same situation; hence his eager-
ness for hunting, and for games of chance. The women are
submitted to unjust drudgery. This I believe is the case with
every barbarous people. With such, force is law. The
stronger sex therefore imposes on the weaker. It is civilization alone which replaces women in the enjoyment of their
natural equality. That first teaches us to subdue the selfish
passions, and to respect those rights in others which we
value in ourselves. Were we in equal barbarism, our females
would be equal drudges. The man with them is less strong
than with us, but their woman stronger than ours; and both
for the same obvious reason; because our man and their
woman is habituated to labour, and formed by it. With both
races the sex which is indulged with ease is least athletic. An
Indian man is small in the hand and wrist for the same
reason for which a sailor is large and strong in the arms and
shoulders, and a porter in the legs and thighs.—They raise
fewer children than we do. The causes of this are to be
found, not in a difference of nature, but of circumstance.
The women very frequently attending the men in their parties of war and of hunting, child-bearing becomes extremely
inconvenient to them. It is said, therefore, that they have
learnt the practice of procuring abortion by the use of some
vegetable; and that it even extends to prevent conception for
a considerable time after. During these parties they are ex-

posed to numerous hazards, to excessive exertions, to the greatest extremities of hunger. Even at their homes the nation depends for food, through a certain part of every year, on the gleanings of the forest: that is, they experience a famine once in every year. With all animals, if the female be badly fed, or not fed at all, her young perish: and if both male and female be reduced to like want, generation becomes less active, less productive. To the obstacles then of want and hazard, which nature has opposed to the multiplication of wild animals, for the purpose of restraining their numbers within certain bounds, those of labour and of voluntary abortion are added with the Indian. No wonder then if they multiply less than we do. Where food is regularly supplied, a single farm will shew more of cattle, than a whole country of forests can of buffaloes. The same Indian women, when married to white traders, who feed them and their children plentifully and regularly, who exempt them from excessive drudgery, who keep them stationary and unexposed to accident, produce and raise as many children as the white women. Instances are known, under these circumstances, of their rearing a dozen children. An inhuman practice once prevailed in this country of making slaves of the Indians. . . .It is a fact well known with us, that the Indian women so enslaved produced and raised as numerous families as either the whites or blacks among whom they lived. —It has been said, that Indians have less hair than the whites, except on the head. But this is a fact of which fair proof can scarcely be had. With them it is disgraceful to be hairy on the body. They say it likens them to hogs. They therefore pluck the hair as fast as it appears. But the traders who marry their women, and prevail on them to discontinue this practice, say, that nature is the same with them as with the whites. Nor, if the fact be true, is the consequence necessary which has been drawn from it. Negroes have notoriously less hair than the whites; yet they are more ardent. But if cold and moisture be the agents of nature for diminishing the races of animals, how comes she all at once to suspend their operation as to the physical man of the new world, whom the Count acknowledges to be "about the same size as the man of our hemisphere," and to let loose their influence on his moral faculties? How has this "combination of the elements and other physical causes, so contrary to the

enlargement of animal nature in this new world, these obstacles to the development and formation of great germs,"
been arrested and suspended, so as to permit the human
body to acquire its just dimensions, and by what inconceiv-
able process has their action been directed on his mind
alone? To judge of the truth of this, to form a just estimate
of their genius and mental powers, more facts are wanting,
and great allowance to be made for those circumstances of
their situation which call for a display of particular talents
only. This done, we shall probably find that they are formed
in mind as well as in body, on the same module with the
"Homo sapiens Europaeus." The principles of their society
forbidding all compulsion, they are to be led to duty and to
enterprize by personal influence and persuasion. Hence eloquence in council, bravery and address in war, become the
foundations of all consequence with them. To these acquire-
ments all their faculties are directed. Of their bravery and
address in war we have multiplied proofs, because we have
been the subjects on which they were exercised. Of their
eminence in oratory we have fewer examples, because it is
displayed chiefly in their own councils. Some, however, we
have of very superior lustre. I may challenge the whole ora-
tions of Demosthenes and Cicero, and of any more eminent
orator, if Europe has furnished more eminent, to produce a
single passage, superior to the speech of Logan, a Mingo
chief, to Lord Dunmore, when governor of this state.[5] And,
as a testimony of their talents in this line, I beg leave to
introduce it, first stating the incidents necessary for understanding it. In the spring of the year 1774, a robbery was
committed by some Indians on certain land-adventurers on
the river Ohio. The whites in that quarter, according to their
custom, undertook to punish this outrage in a summary way.
Captain Michael Cresap, and a certain Daniel Great-house,
leading on these parties, surprized, at different times, tra-
velling and hunting parties of the Indians, having their
women and children with them, and murdered many.
Among these were unfortunately the family of Logan, a chief
celebrated in peace and war, and long distinguished as the
friend of the whites. This unworthy return provoked his

[5]On the Logan affair see the Appendix in Peden's edition of the
Notes, pp. 226–258, 274–5.—*Editor*

vengeance. He accordingly signalized himself in the war which ensued. In the autumn of the same year a decisive battle was fought at the mouth of the Great Kanhaway, between the collected forces of the Shawanese, Mingoes, and Delawares, and a detachment of the Virginia militia. The Indians were defeated, and sued for peace. Logan however disdained to be seen among the suppliants. But, lest the sincerity of a treaty should be distrusted, from which so distinguished a chief absented himself, he sent by a messenger the following speech to be delivered to Lord Dunmore.

"I appeal to any white man to say, if ever he entered Logan's cabin hungry, and he gave him not meat; if ever he came cold and naked, and he clothed him not. During the course of the last long and bloody war, Logan remained idle in his cabin, an advocate for peace. Such was my love for the whites, that my countrymen pointed as they passed, and said, 'Logan is the friend of white men.' I had even thought to have lived with you, but for the injuries of one man. Col. Cresap, the last spring, in cold blood, and unprovoked, murdered all the relations of Logan, not sparing even my women and children. There runs not a drop of my blood in the veins of any living creature. This called on me for revenge. I have sought it: I have killed many: I have fully glutted my vengeance. For my country, I rejoice at the beams of peace. But do not harbour a thought that mine is the joy of fear. Logan never felt fear. He will not turn on his heel to save his life. Who is there to mourn for Logan?—Not one."

Before we condemn the Indians of this continent as wanting genius, we must consider that letters have not yet been introduced among them. Were we to compare them in their present state with the Europeans North of the Alps, when the Roman arms and arts first crossed those mountains, the comparison would be unequal, because, at that time, those parts of Europe were swarming with numbers; because numbers produce emulation, and multiply the chances of improvement, and one improvement begets another. Yet I may safely ask, How many good poets, how many able mathematicians, how many great inventors in arts or sciences, had Europe North of the Alps then produced? And it was sixteen centuries after this before a Newton could be formed. I do not mean to deny, that there are varieties in the race of man, distinguished by their powers both of body and mind. I believe there are, as I see to be the case in the races of other animals. I only mean to suggest a doubt, whether the bulk and faculties of animals depend on the side of the Atlantic on which their food happens to grow, or which furnishes the elements of which they are compounded? Whether nature has enlisted herself as a Cis or Trans-Atlantic partisan? I am induced to suspect, there has been more eloquence than sound reasoning displayed in support of this theory; that it is one of those cases where the judgment has been seduced by a glowing pen: and whilst I render every tribute of honor and esteem to the celebrated Zoologist, who has added, and is still adding, so many precious things to the treasures of science, I must doubt whether in this instance he has not cherished error also, by lending her for a moment his vivid imagination and bewitching language.

So far the Count de Buffon has carried this new theory of the tendency of nature to belittle her productions on this side of the Atlantic. Its application to the race of whites, transplanted from Europe, remained for the Abbé Raynal. "One must be astonished (he says) that America has not yet produced one good poet, one able mathematician, one man of genius in a single art or a single science."[6] "America has not yet produced one good poet." When we shall have existed as a people as long as the Greeks did before they produced a Homer, the Romans a Virgil, the French a Racine and Voltaire, the English a Shakespeare and Milton, should this reproach be still true, we will enquire from what unfriendly causes it has proceeded, that the other countries of Europe and quarters of the earth shall not have inscribed any name in the roll of poets. But neither has America produced "one able mathematician, one man of genius in a single art or a single science." In war we have produced a Washington, whose memory will be adored while liberty shall have votaries, whose name will triumph over time, and will in future ages assume its just station among the most celebrated worthies of the world, when that wretched philosophy shall be forgotten which would have arranged him among the degeneracies of nature. In physics we have pro-

[6]Guillaume Thomas Francois Raynal, *Histoire Philosophique et Politique des Établissemens et du Commerce des Européens dans les deux Indes,* 4 vols. Amsterdam, 1770.

duced a Franklin, than whom no one of the present age has
made more important discoveries, nor has enriched philosophy with more, or more ingenious solutions of the pha-
enomena of nature. We have supposed Mr. Rittenhouse
second to no astronomer living: that in genius he must be
the first, because he is self-taught. As an artist he has exhib-
ited as great a proof of mechanical genius as the world has
ever produced. He has not indeed made a world; but he has
by imitation approached nearer its Maker than any man who
has lived from the creation to this day.[7] As in philosophy and
war, so in government, in oratory, in painting, in the plastic
art, we might shew that America, though but a child of yes-
terday, has already given hopeful proofs of genius, as well
of the nobler kinds, which arouse the best feelings of man,
which call him into action, which substantiate his freedom,
and conduct him to happiness, as of the subordinate, which
serve to amuse him only. We therefore suppose, that this
reproach is as unjust as it is unkind; and that, of the geniuses
which adorn the present age, America contributes its full
share. For comparing it with those countries, where genius
is most cultivated, where are the most excellent models for
art, and scaffoldings for the attainment of science, as France
and England for instance, we calculate thus. The United
States contain three millions of inhabitants; France twenty
millions; and the British islands ten. We produce a Washington, a Franklin, a Rittenhouse. France then should have half
a dozen in each of these lines, and Great-Britain half that
number, equally eminent. It may be true, that France has: we
are but just becoming acquainted with her, and our ac-
quaintance so far gives us high ideas of the genius of her
inhabitants. It would be injuring too many of them to name
particularly a Voltaire, a Buffon, the constellation of Ency-
clopedists, the Abbé Raynal himself, &c. &c. We therefore
have reason to believe she can produce her full quota of
genius. The present war having so long cut off all communi-
cation with Great-Britain, we are not able to make a fair
estimate of the state of science in that country. The spirit in
which she wages war is the only sample before our eyes, and
that does not seem the legitimate offspring either of science

[7]David Rittenhouse (1732–1796) of Philadelphia, artisan, mathematician and astronomer.—*Editor*

or of civilization. The sun of her glory is fast descending to the horizon. Her philosophy has crossed the Channel, her freedom the Atlantic, and herself seems passing to that awful dissolution, whose issue is not given human foresight to scan. . . .

Query VII: Population[8]

. . . But are there no inconveniences to be thrown into the scale against the advantage expected from a multiplication of numbers by the importation of foreigners? It is for the happiness of those united in society to harmonize as much as possible in matters which they must of necessity transact together. Civil government being the sole object of forming societies, its administration must be conducted by common consent. Every species of government has its specific principles. Ours perhaps are more peculiar than those of any other in the universe. It is a composition of the freest principles of the English constitution, with others derived from natural right and natural reason. To these nothing can be more opposed than the maxims of absolute monarchies. Yet, from such, we are to expect the greatest number of emigrants. They will bring with them the principles of the governments they leave, imbibed in their early youth; or, if able to throw them off, it will be in exchange for an unbounded licentiousness, passing, as is usual, from one extreme to another. It would be a miracle were they to stop precisely at the point of temperate liberty. These principles, with their language, they will transmit to their children. In proportion to their numbers, they will share with us the legislation. They will infuse into it their spirit, warp and bias its direction, and render it a heterogeneous, incoherent, distracted mass. I may appeal to experience, during the present contest, for a verification of these conjectures. But, if they be not certain

[8]Jefferson considers whether it is good policy for America to increase its population by immigration. After calculating that America can double its population every twenty-seven and a quarter years without immigration, he speaks of the need for a homogeneous population, even, or especially, in a free society. Then he comments on the importation of slaves.—*Editor*

in event, are they not possible, are they not probable? Is i̇̇
not safer to wait with patience 27 years and three months
longer, for the attainment of any degree of population desired, or expected? May not our government be more homogeneous, more peaceable, more durable? Suppose 20
millions of republican Americans thrown all of a sudden into
France, what would be the condition of that kingdom? If it
would be more turbulent, less happy, less strong, we may
believe that the addition of half a million of foreigners to our
present numbers would produce a similar effect here. If they
come of themselves, they are entitled to all the rights of
citizenship: but I doubt the expediency of inviting them by
extraordinary encouragements. I mean not that these
doubts should be extended to the importation of useful
artificers. The policy of that measure depends on very different considerations. Spare no expence in obtaining them.
They will after a while go to the plough and the hoe; but, in
the mean time, they will teach us something we do not know.
It is not so in agriculture. The indifferent state of that among
us does not proceed from a want of knowledge merely; it is
from our having such quantities of land to waste as we
please. In Europe the object is to make the most of their
land, labour being abundant: here it is to make the most of
our labour, land being abundant. . . .

. . . Under the mild treatment our slaves experience, and
their wholesome, though coarse, food, this blot in our country increases as fast, or faster, than the whites. During the
regal government, we had at one time obtained a law, which
imposed such a duty on the importation of slaves, as
amounted nearly to a prohibition, when one inconsiderate
assembly, placed under a peculiarity of circumstance, repealed the law. This repeal met a joyful sanction from the
then sovereign, and no devices, no expedients, which could
ever after be attempted by subsequent assemblies, and they
seldom met without attempting them, could succeed in getting the royal assent to a renewal of the duty. In the very first
session held under the republican government, the assembly passed a law for the perpetual prohibition of the importation of slaves. This will in some measure stop the increase
of this great political and moral evil, while the minds of our
citizens may be ripening for a complete emancipation of
human nature.

Query XI: Aborigines[9]

... This practice results from the circumstance of their having never submitted themselves to any laws, any coercive power, any shadow of government. Their only controuls are their manners, and that moral sense of right and wrong, which, like the sense of tasting and feeling, in every man makes a part of his nature. An offence against these is punished by contempt, by exclusion from society, or, where the case is serious, as that of murder, by the individuals whom it concerns. Imperfect as this species of coercion may seem, crimes are very rare among them: insomuch that were it made a question, whether no law, as among the savage Americans, or too much law, as among the civilized Europeans, submits man to the greatest evil, one who has seen both conditions of existence would pronounce it to be the last: and that the sheep are happier of themselves, than under care of the wolves. It will be said, that great societies cannot exist without government. The Savages therefore break them into small ones. . . .

Query XIII: Constitution[10]

... This constitution was formed when we were new and unexperienced in the science of government. It was the first too which was formed in the whole United States. No wonder then that time and trial have discovered very capital defects in it.

1. The majority of the men in the state, who pay and fight for its support, are unrepresented in the legislature, the roll of freeholders intitled to vote, not including generally the half of those on the roll of the militia, or of the tax-gatherers.

2. Among those who share the representation, the shares are very unequal. Thus the county of Warwick, with only one

[9]More on Indians: Jefferson explains why they have "separated into so many little societies."—*Editor*
[10]Having detailed the various royal charters under which English colonists had come to Virginia, Jefferson summarizes Virginia's first independent constitution of 1776 and sets forth its defects. —*Editor*

hundred fighting men, has an equal representation with the county of Loudon, which has 1746. So that every man in Warwick has as much influence in the government as 17 men in Loudon. But lest it should be thought that an equal interspersion of small among large counties, through the whole state, may prevent any danger of injury to particular parts of it, we will divide it into districts, and shew the proportions of land, of fighting men, and of representation in each.

An inspection of this table will supply the place of commentaries on it. It will appear at once that nineteen thousand men,[11] living below the falls of the rivers, possess half the senate, and want four members only of possessing a majority of the house of delegates; a want more than supplied by the vicinity of their situation to the seat of government, and of course the greater degree of convenience and punctuality with which their members may and will attend in the legislature. These nineteen thousand, therefore, living in one part of the country, give law to upwards of thirty thousand, living in another, and appoint all their chief officers, executive and judiciary. From the difference of their situation and circumstances, their interests will often be very different.

3. The senate is, by its constitution, too homogeneous with the house of delegates. Being chosen by the same electors, at the same time, and out of the same subjects, the choice falls of course on men of the same description. The

	Square miles	Fighting men	Delegates	Senators
Between the sea-coast and falls of the rivers	11,205	19,012	71	12
Between the falls of the rivers and the Blue ridge of mountains	18,759	18,828	46	8
Between the Blue ridge and the Alleghaney	11,911	7,673	16	2
Between the Alleghaney and Ohio	79,650	4,458	16	2
Total	121,525	49,971	149	24

[11]Note that Jefferson, in accordance with the Virginia Constitution of 1776 and his own Draft Constitution of 1783, counts "fighting men" as electors.—Editor

purpose of establishing different houses of legislation is to introduce the influence of different interests or different principles. Thus in Great-Britain it is said their constitution relies on the house of commons for honesty, and the lords for wisdom; which would be a rational reliance if honesty were to be bought with money, and if wisdom were heredi- tary. In some of the American states the delegates and sena- tors are so chosen, as that the first represent the persons, and the second the property of the state. But with us, wealth and wisdom have equal chance for admission into both houses. We do not therefore derive from the separation of our legislature into two houses, those benefits which a proper complication of principles is capable of producing, and those which alone can compensate the evils which may be produced by their dissensions.

4. All the powers of government, legislative, executive, and judiciary, result to the legislative body. The concentrat- ing these in the same hands is precisely the definition of despotic government. It will be no alleviation that these powers will be exercised by a plurality of hands, and not by a single one. 173 despots would surely be as oppressive as one. Let those who doubt it turn their eyes on the republic of Venice. As little will it avail us that they are chosen by ourselves. An *elective despotism* was not the government we fought for; but one which should not only be founded on free principles, but in which the powers of government should be so divided and balanced among several bodies of magistracy, as that no one could transcend their legal limits, without being effectually checked and restrained by the oth- ers. For this reason that convention, which passed the ordi- nance of government, laid its foundation on this basis, that the legislative, executive and judiciary department should be separate and distinct, so that no person should exercise the powers of more than one of them at the same time. But no barrier was provided between these several powers. The judiciary and executive members were left dependant on the legislative, for their subsistence in office, and some of them for their continuance in it. If therefore the legislature as- sumes executive and judiciary powers, no opposition is likely to be made; nor, if made, can it be effectual; because in that case they may put their proceedings into the form of an act of assembly, which will render them obligatory on the

other branches. They have accordingly, in many instances, decided rights which should have been left to judiciary controversy: and the direction of the executive, during the whole time of their session, is becoming habitual and familiar. And this is done with no ill intention. The views of the present members are perfectly upright. When they are led out of their regular province, it is by art in others, and inadvertence in themselves. And this will probably be the case for some time to come. But it will not be a very long time. Mankind soon learn to make interested uses of every right and power which they possess, or may assume. The public money and public liberty, intended to have been deposited with three branches of magistracy, but found inadvertently to be in the hands of one only, will soon be discovered to be sources of wealth and dominion to those who hold them; distinguished too by this tempting circumstance, that they are the instrument, as well as the object of acquisition. With money we will get men, said Caesar, and with men we will get money. Nor should our assembly be deluded by the integrity of their own purposes, and conclude that these unlimited powers will never be abused, because themselves are not disposed to abuse them. They should look forward to a time, and that not a distant one, when corruption in this, as in the country from which we derive our origin, will have seized the heads of government, and be spread by them through the body of the people; when they will purchase the voices of the people, and make them pay the price. Human nature is the same on every side of the Atlantic, and will be alike influenced by the same causes. The time to guard against corruption and tyranny, is before they shall have gotten hold on us. It is better to keep the wolf out of the fold, than to trust to drawing his teeth and talons after he shall have entered. To render these considerations the more cogent, we must observe in addition,

5. That the ordinary legislature may alter the constitution itself. On the discontinuance of assemblies, it became necessary to substitute in their place some other body, competent to the ordinary business of government, and to the calling forth the powers of the state for the maintenance of our opposition to Great-Britain. Conventions were therefore introduced, consisting of two delegates from each county,

meeting together and forming one house, on the plan of the former house of Burgesses, to whose places they succeeded. These were at first chosen anew for every particular session. But in March 1775, they recommended to the people to chuse a convention, which should continue in office a year. This was done accordingly in April 1775, and in the July following that convention passed an ordinance for the election of delegates in the month of April annually. It is well known, that in July 1775, a separation from Great-Britain and establishment of Republican government had never yet entered into any person's mind. A convention therefore, chosen under that ordinance, cannot be said to have been chosen for purposes which certainly did not exist in the minds of those who passed it. Under this ordinance, at the annual election in April 1776, a convention for the year was chosen. Independence, and the establishment of a new form of government, were not even yet the objects of the people at large. One extract from the pamphlet called Common Sense[12] had appeared in the Virginia papers in February, and copies of the pamphlet itself had got into a few hands. But the idea had not been opened to the mass of the people in April, much less can it be said that they had made up their minds in its favor. So that the electors of April 1776, no more than the legislators of July 1775, not thinking of independance and a permanent republic, could not mean to vest in these delegates powers of establishing them, or any authorities other than those of the ordinary legislature. So far as a temporary organization of government was necessary to render our opposition energetic, so far their organization was valid. But they received in their creation no powers but what were given to every legislature before and since. They could not therefore pass an act transcendant to the powers of other legislatures. If the present assembly pass any act, and declare it shall be irrevocable by subsequent assemblies, the declaration is merely void, and the act repealable, as other acts are. So far, and no farther authorized, they organized the government by the ordinance entitled a Constitution or Form of government. It pretends to no higher authority than the other ordinances of the same session; it does not say, that it shall be perpetual; that it shall

[12]Written by Tom Paine—*Editor*

be unalterable by other legislatures; that it shall be transcendant above the powers of those, who they knew would
have equal power with themselves. Not only the silence of
the instrument is a proof they thought it would be alterable,
but their own practice also: for this very convention, meeting as a House of Delegates in General Assembly with the
new Senate in the autumn of that year, passed acts of assembly in contradiction to their ordinance of government; and
every assembly from that time to this has done the same. I
am safe therefore in the position, that the constitution itself
is alterable by the ordinary legislature. . . .

In enumerating the defects of the constitution, it would be
wrong to count among them what is only the error of particular persons. In December 1776, our circumstances being
much distressed, it was proposed in the house of delegates
to create a *dictator,* invested with every power legislative,
executive and judiciary, civil and military, of life and of
death, over our persons and over our properties: and in June
1781, again under calamity, the same proposition was repeated, and wanted a few votes only of being passed.—One
who entered into this contest from a pure love of liberty, and
a sense of injured rights, who determined to make every
sacrifice, and to meet every danger, for the re-establishment
of those rights on a firm basis, who did not mean to expend
his blood and substance for the wretched purpose of changing this master for that, but to place the powers of governing
him in a plurality of hands of his own choice, so that the
corrupt will of no one man might in future oppress him,
must stand confounded and dismayed when he is told that
a considerable portion of that plurality had meditated the
surrender of them into a single hand, and, in lieu of a limited
monarch, to deliver him over to a despotic one! How must
we find his efforts and sacrifices abused and baffled, if he
may still by a single vote be laid prostrate at the feet of one
man! In God's name, from whence have they derived this
power? Is it from our ancient laws? None such can be produced. Is it from any principle in our new constitution, expressed or implied? Every lineament of that expressed or
implied, is in full opposition to it. Its fundamental principle
is, that the state shall be governed as a commonwealth. It
provides a republican organization, proscribes under the
name of *prerogative* the exercise of all powers undefined by

the laws; places on this basis the whole system of our laws; and, by consolidating them together, chuses that they shall be left to stand or fall together, never providing for any circumstances, nor admitting that such could arise, wherein either should be suspended, no, not for a moment. Our antient laws expressly declare, that those who are but delegates themselves shall not delegate to others powers which require judgment and integrity in their exercise.—Or was this proposition moved on a supposed right in the movers of abandoning their posts in a moment of distress? The same laws forbid the abandonment of that post, even on ordinary occasions; and much more a transfer of their powers into other hands and other forms, without consulting the people. They never admit the idea that these, like sheep or cattle, may be given from hand to hand without an appeal to their own will.—Was it from the necessity of the case? Necessities which dissolve a government, do not convey its authority to an oligarchy or a monarchy. They throw back, into the hands of the people, the powers they had delegated, and leave them as individuals to shift for themselves. A leader may offer, but not impose himself, nor be imposed on them. Much less can their necks be submitted to his sword, their breath be held at his will or caprice. The necessity which should operate these tremendous effects should at least be palpable and irresistible. Yet in both instances, where it was feared, or pretended with us, it was belied by the event. It was belied too by the preceding experience of our sister states, several of whom had grappled through greater difficulties without abandoning their forms of government. When the proposition was first made, Massachusets had found even the government of committees sufficient to carry them through an invasion. But we at the time of that proposition were under no invasion. When the second was made, there had been added to this example those of Rhode-Island, New-York, New-Jersey, and Pennsylvania, in all of which the republican form had been found equal to the task of carrying them through the severest trials. In this state alone did there exist so little virtue, that fear was to be fixed in the hearts of the people, and to become the motive of their exertions and the principle of their government? The very thought alone was treason against the people; was treason against mankind in general; as rivetting for ever the chains which bow down their necks, by giving to their oppressors a proof, which they would have trumpeted through the universe, of the imbecility of republican government, in times of pressing danger, to shield them from harm. Those who assume the right of giving away the reins of government in any case, must be sure that the herd, whom they hand on to the rods and hatchet of the dictator, will lay their necks on the block when he shall nod to them. But if our assemblies supposed such a resignation in the people, I hope they mistook their character. I am of opinion, that the government, instead of being braced and invigorated for greater exertions under their difficulties, would have been thrown back upon the bungling machinery of county committees for administration, till a convention could have been called, and its wheels again set into regular motion. What a cruel moment was this for creating such an embarrassment, for putting to the proof the attachment of our countrymen to republican government! Those who meant well, of the advocates for this measure, (and most of them meant well, for I know them personally, had been their fellow-labourers in the common cause, and had often proved the purity of their principles), had been seduced in their judgment by the example of an ancient republic, whose constitution and circumstances were fundamentally different. They had sought this precedent in the history of Rome, where alone it was to be found, and where at length too it had proved fatal. They had taken it from a republic, rent by the most bitter factions and tumults, where the government was of a heavy-handed unfeeling aristocracy, over a people ferocious, and rendered desperate by poverty and wretchedness; tumults which could not be allayed under the most trying circumstances, but by the omnipotent hand of a single despot. Their constitution therefore allowed a temporary tyrant to be erected, under the name of a Dictator; and that temporary tyrant, after a few examples, became perpetual. They misapplied this precedent to a people, mild in their dispositions, patient under their trial, united for the public liberty, and affectionate to their leaders. But if from the constitution of the Roman government there resulted to their Senate a power of submitting all their rights to the will of one man, does it follow, that the assembly of Virginia have the same authority? What clause in our constitution has substituted that of

Rome, by way of residuary provision, for all cases not otherwise provided for? Or if they may step *ad libitum* into any
other form of government for precedents to rule us by, for
what oppression may not a precedent be found in this world
of the *bellum omnium in omnia?*[13]— Searching for the foundations of this proposition, I can find none which may pretend
a colour of right or reason, but the defect before developed,
that there being no barrier between the legislative, executive, and judiciary departments, the legislature may seize the
whole: that having seized it, and possessing a right to fix
their own quorum, they may reduce that quorum to one,
whom they may call a chairman, speaker, dictator, or by any
other name they please.—Our situation is indeed perilous,
and I hope my countrymen will be sensible of it, and will
apply, at a proper season, the proper remedy; which is a
convention to fix the constitution, to amend its defects, to
bind up the several branches of government by certain laws,
which when they transgress their acts shall become nullities;
to render unnecessary an appeal to the people, or in other
words a rebellion, on every infraction of their rights, on the
peril that their acquiescence shall be construed into an intention to surrender those rights.

Query XIV: Laws[14]

. . . to emancipate all slaves born after passing the act. The
bill reported by the revisors does not itself contain this proposition; but an amendment containing it was prepared, to be
offered to the legislature whenever the bill should be taken
up, and further directing, that they should continue with
their parents to a certain age, then be brought up, at the
public expense, to tillage, arts or sciences, according to their
geniusses, till the females should be eighteen, and the males

[13]"the war of all against all things"—*Editor*
[14]Jefferson describes Virginia's laws and then a planned revision
of them drawn up by "three gentlemen"—one of them himself,
though he does not say so—to make them "republican." To justify
a radical revision that would emancipate slaves, Jefferson launches
into a long discussion of Blacks, their nature and the reasons why
they should be sent away to colonies after they are set free.—
Editor

twenty-one years of age, when they should be colonized to such place as the circumstances of the time should render most proper, sending them out with arms, implements of houshold and of the handicraft arts, seeds, pairs of the useful domestic animals, &c. to declare them a free and independant people, and extend to them our alliance and protection, till they shall have acquired strength; and to send vessels at the same time to other parts of the world for an equal number of white inhabitants; to induce whom to migrate hither, proper encouragements were to be proposed. It will probably be asked, Why not retain and incorporate the blacks into the state, and thus save the expence of supplying, by importation of white settlers, the vacancies they will leave? Deep rooted prejudices entertained by the whites; ten thousand recollections, by the blacks, of the injuries they have sustained; new provocations; the real distinctions which nature has made; and many other circumstances, will divide us into parties, and produce convulsions which will probably never end but in the extermination of the one or the other race.—To these objections, which are political, may be added others, which are physical and moral. The first difference which strikes us is that of colour. Whether the black of the negro resides in the reticular membrane between the skin and scarf-skin, or in the scarf-skin itself; whether it proceeds from the colour of the blood, the colour of the bile, or from that of some other secretion, the difference is fixed in nature, and is as real as if its seat and cause were better known to us. And is this difference of no importance? Is it not the foundation of a greater or less share of beauty in the two races? Are not the fine mixtures of red and white, the expressions of every passion by greater or less suffusions of colour in the one, preferable to that eternal monotony, which reigns in the countenances, that immoveable veil of black which covers all the emotions of the other race? Add to these, flowing hair, a more elegant symmetry of form, their own judgment in favour of the whites, declared by their preference of them, as uniformly as is the preference of the Oran-ootan for the black women over those of his own species. The circumstance of superior beauty, is thought worthy attention in the propagation of our horses, dogs, and other domestic animals; why not in that of man? Besides those of colour, figure, and hair, there are other physical distinctions proving a difference of race. They have less hair on the face and body. They secrete less by the kidneys, and more by the glands of the skin, which gives them a very strong and disagreeable odour. This greater degree of transpiration renders them more tolerant of heat, and less so of cold, than the whites. Perhaps too a difference of structure in the pulmonary apparatus, which a late ingenious experimentalist[15] has discovered to be the principal regulator of animal heat, may have disabled them from extricating, in the act of inspiration, so much of that fluid from the outer air, or obliged them in expiration, to part with more of it. They seem to require less sleep. A black, after hard labour through the day, will be induced by the slightest amusements to sit up till midnight, or later, though knowing he must be out with the first dawn of the morning. They are at least as brave, and more adventuresome. But this may perhaps proceed from a want of forethought, which prevents their seeing a danger till it be present. When present, they do not go through it with more coolness or steadiness than the whites. They are more ardent after their female: but love seems with them to be more an eager desire, than a tender delicate mixture of sentiment and sensation. Their griefs are transient. Those numberless afflictions, which render it doubtful whether heaven has given life to us in mercy or in wrath, are less felt, and sooner forgotten with them. In general, their existence appears to participate more of sensation than reflection. To this must be ascribed their disposition to sleep when abstracted from their diversions, and unemployed in labour. An animal whose body is at rest, and who does not reflect, must be disposed to sleep of course. Comparing them by their faculties of memory, reason, and imagination, it appears to me, that in memory they are equal to the whites; in reason much inferior, as I think one could scarcely be found capable of tracing and comprehending the investigations of Euclid; and that in imagination they are dull, tasteless, and anomalous. It would be unfair to follow them to Africa for this investigation. We will consider them here, on the same stage with the whites, and where the facts are not apocryphal on which a judgment is to be formed. It will be right to make great

[15]Adair Crawford (1748–1795), author of *Experiments and Observations on Animal Heat.* London, 1779.—*Editor*

allowances for the difference of condition, of education, of conversation, of the sphere in which they move. Many millions of them have been brought to, and born in America. Most of them indeed have been confined to tillage, to their own homes, and their own society: yet many have been so situated, that they might have availed themselves of the conversation of their masters; many have been brought up to the handicraft arts, and from that circumstance have always been associated with the whites. Some have been liberally educated, and all have lived in countries where the arts and sciences are cultivated to a considerable degree, and have had before their eyes samples of the best works from abroad. The Indians, with no advantages of this kind, will often carve figures on their pipes not destitute of design and merit. They will crayon out an animal, a plant, or a country, so as to prove the existence of a germ in their minds which only wants cultivation. They astonish you with strokes of the most sublime oratory; such as prove their reason and sentiment strong, their imagination glowing and elevated. But never yet could I find that a black had uttered a thought above the level of plain narration; never see even an elementary trait of painting or sculpture. In music they are more generally gifted than the whites with accurate ears for tune and time, and they have been found capable of imagining a small catch. Whether they will be equal to the composition of a more extensive run of melody, or of complicated harmony, is yet to be proved. Misery is often the parent of the most affecting touches in poetry.—Among the blacks is misery enough, God knows, but no poetry. Love is the peculiar oestrum of the poet. Their love is ardent, but it kindles the senses only, not the imagination. Religion indeed has produced a Phyllis Whatley;[16] but it could not produce a poet. The compositions published under her name are below the dignity of criticism. The heroes of the Dunciad are to her, as Hercules to the author of that poem. Ignatius Sancho[17] has approached nearer to merit in composition; yet his letters do more honour to the heart than the head. They

---

[16]Phyllis Wheatley (ca. 1753–1784), an African-born servant, author of *Poems on Various Subjects, Religious and Moral.* London, 1773.—*Editor*

[17]Ignatius Sancho (1729–1780), author of *Letters.* London, 1782.—*Editor*

breathe the purest effusions of friendship and general philanthropy, and shew how great a degree of the latter may be
compounded with strong religious zeal. He is often happy
in the turn of his compliments, and his stile is easy and
familiar, except when he effects a Shandean fabrication of
words. But his imagination is wild and extravagant, escapes
incessantly from every restraint of reason and taste, and, in
the course of its vagaries, leaves a tract of thought as incoherent and eccentric, as is the course of a meteor through
the sky. His subjects should often have led him to a process
of sober reasoning: yet we find him always substituting sentiment for demonstration. Upon the whole, though we admit
him to the first place among those of his own colour who
have presented themselves to the public judgment, yet when
we compare him with the writers of the race among whom
he lived, and particularly with the epistolary class, in which
he has taken his own stand, we are compelled to enroll him
at the bottom of the column. This criticism supposes the
letters published under his name to be genuine, and to have
received amendment from no other hand; points which
would not be of easy investigation. The improvement of the
blacks in body and mind, in the first instance of their mixture
with the whites, has been observed by every one, and proves
that their inferiority is not the effect merely of their condition of life. We know that among the Romans, about the
Augustan age especially, the condition of their slaves was
much more deplorable than that of the blacks on the continent of America. The two sexes were confined in separate
apartments, because to raise a child cost the master more
than to buy one. Cato, for a very restricted indulgence to his
slaves in this particular, took from them a certain price.[18]
But in this country the slaves multiply as fast as the free
inhabitants. Their situation and manners place the commerce between the two sexes almost without restraint.—The
same Cato, on a principle of oeconomy, always sold his sick
and superannuated slaves. He gives it as a standing precept
to a master visiting his farm, to sell his old oxen, old wag-
gons, old tools, old and diseased servants, and every thing
else become useless. *"Vendat boves vetulos, plaustrum vetus, fer-
ramenta, vetera, servum senem, servum morbosum, & si quid aliud*

[18]Plutarch, *Life of Cato,* 21.

supersit vendat. "[19] The American slaves cannot enumerate this among the injuries and insults they receive. It was the common practice to expose in the island of Aesculapius, in the Tyber, diseased slaves, whose cure was like to become tedious.[20] The Emperor Claudius, by an edict, gave freedom to such of them as should recover, and first declared, that if any person chose to kill rather than to expose them, it should be deemed homicide. The exposing them is a crime of which no instance has existed with us; and were it to be followed by death, it would be punished capitally. We are told of a certain Vedius Pollio, who, in the presence of Augustus, would have given a slave as food to his fish, for having broken a glass.[21] With the Romans, the regular method of taking the evidence of their slaves was under torture. Here it has been thought better never to resort to their evidence. When a master was murdered, all his slaves, in the same house, or within hearing, were condemned to death. Here punishment falls on the guilty only, and as precise proof is required against him as against a freeman. Yet notwithstanding these and other discouraging circumstances among the Romans, their slaves were often their rarest artists. They excelled too in science, insomuch as to be usually employed as tutors to their master's children. Epictetus, (Diogenes, Phaedon), Terence, and Phaedrus, were slaves. But they were of the race of whites. It is not their condition then, but nature, which has produced the distinction.—Whether further observation will or will not verify the conjecture, that nature has been less bountiful to them in the endowments of the head, I believe that in those of the heart she will be found to have done them justice. That disposition to theft with which they have been branded, must be ascribed to their situation, and not to any depravity of the moral sense. The man, in whose favour no laws of property exist, probably feels himself less bound to respect those made in favour of others. When arguing for ourselves, we lay it down as a fundamental, that laws, to be just, must give a

---

[19]Cato, *De re rustica,* 2; the translation appears in the preceding sentence.—*Editor*
[20]Suetonius, *Life of Claudius,* 25.
[21]Seneca, *De Ira,* 3.40, *De Clementia,* 1.18; Jean Xiphilin, *L'Abregé de Dion Cassius,* Augustus, 76.

reciprocation of right: that, without this, they are mere arbitrary rules of conduct, founded in force, and not in conscience: and it is a problem which I give to the master to solve, whether the religious precepts against the violation of property were not framed for him as well as his slave? And whether the slave may not as justifiably take a little from one, who has taken all from him, as he may slay one who would slay him? That a change in the relations in which a man is placed should change his ideas of moral right and wrong, is neither new, nor peculiar to the colour of the blacks. Homer tells us it was so 2600 years ago.

> Jove fix'd it certain, that whatever day
> Makes man a slave, takes half his worth away.[22]

But the slaves of which Homer speaks were whites. Notwithstanding these considerations which must weaken their respect for the laws of property, we find among them numerous instances of the most rigid integrity, and as many as among their better instructed masters, of benevolence, gratitude, and unshaken fidelity.—The opinion, that they are inferior in the faculties of reason and imagination, must be hazarded with great diffidence. To justify a general conclusion, requires many observations, even where the subject may be submitted to the Anatomical knife, to Optical glasses, to analysis by fire, or by solvents. How much more then where it is a faculty, not a substance, we are examining; where it eludes the research of all the senses; where the conditions of its existence are various and variously combined; where the effects of those which are present or absent bid defiance to calculation; let me add too, as a circumstance of great tenderness, where our conclusion would degrade a whole race of men from the rank in the scale of beings which their Creator may perhaps have given them. To our reproach it must be said, that though for a century and a half we have had under our eyes the races of black and of red men, they have never yet been viewed by us as subjects of natural history. I advance it therefore as a suspicion only, that the blacks, whether originally a distinct race, or made distinct by time and circumstances, are inferior to the whites in the endowments both of body and mind. It is not against

[22] *Odyssey*, XVII, 392-3, in the Pope translation. Jefferson also quotes the Greek.—*Editor*

experience to suppose, that different species of the same genus, or varieties of the same species, may possess different qualifications. Will not a lover of natural history then, one who views the gradations in all the races of animals with the eye of philosophy, excuse an effort to keep those in the department of man as distinct as nature has formed them? This unfortunate difference of colour, and perhaps of faculty, is a powerful obstacle to the emancipation of these people. Many of their advocates, while they wish to vindicate the liberty of human nature, are anxious also to preserve its dignity and beauty. Some of these, embarrassed by the question "What further is to be done with them?" join themselves in opposition with those who are actuated by sordid avarice only. Among the Romans emancipation required but one effort. The slave, when made free, might mix with, without staining the blood of his master. But with us a second is necessary, unknown to history. When freed, he is to be removed beyond the reach of mixture. . . .

Another object of the revisal is, to diffuse knowledge more generally through the mass of the people.[23] This bill proposes to lay off every county into small districts of five or six miles square, called hundreds, and in each of them to establish a school for teaching reading, writing, and arithmetic. The tutor to be supported by the hundred, and every person in it entitled to send their children three years gratis, and as much longer as they please, paying for it. These schools to be under a visitor, who is annually to chuse the boy, of best genius in the school, of those whose parents are too poor to give them further education, and to send him forward to one of the grammar schools, of which twenty are proposed to be erected in different parts of the country, for teaching Greek, Latin, geography, and the higher branches of numerical arithmetic. Of the boys thus sent in any one year, trial is to be made at the grammar schools one or two years, and the best genius of the whole selected, and continued six years, and the residue dismissed. By this means twenty of the best geniusses will be raked from the rubbish annually, and be instructed, at the public expence, so far as the grammar

[23]Another item of the revision or "revisal" is education. Jefferson's "Bill for the More General Diffusion of Knowledge" never passed, but his defense of it shows what kind of popular education he thought necessary to sustain republican government.—*Editor*

schools go. At the end of six years instruction, one half are to be discontinued (from among whom the grammar schools will probably be supplied with future masters); and the other half, who are to be chosen for the superiority of their parts and disposition, are to be sent and continued three years in the study of such sciences as they shall chuse, at William and Mary college, the plan of which is proposed to be enlarged, as will be hereafter explained, and extended to all the useful sciences. The ultimate result of the whole scheme of education would be the teaching all children of the state reading, writing, and common arithmetic: turning out ten annually of superior genius, well taught in Greek, Latin, geography, and the higher branches of arithmetic: turning out ten others annually, of still superior parts, who, to those branches of learning, shall have added such of the sciences as their genius shall have led them to: the furnishing to the wealthier part of the people convenient schools, at which their children may be educated, at their own expence.—The general objects of this law are to provide an education adapted to the years, to the capacity, and the condition of every one, and directed to their freedom and happiness. Specific details were not proper for the law. These must be the business of the visitors entrusted with its execution. The first stage of this education being the schools of the hundreds, wherein the great mass of the people will receive their instruction, the principal foundations of future order will be laid here. Instead therefore of putting the Bible and Testament into the hands of the children, at an age when their judgments are not sufficiently matured for religious enquiries, their memories may here be stored with the most useful facts from Grecian, Roman, European and American history. The first elements of morality too may be instilled into their minds; such as, when further developed as their judgments advance in strength, may teach them how to work out their own greatest happiness, by shewing them that it does not depend on the condition of life in which chance has placed them, but is always the result of a good conscience, good health, occupation, and freedom in all just pursuits.—Those whom either the wealth of their parents or the adoption of the state shall destine to higher degrees of learning, will go on to the grammar schools, which constitute the next stage, there to be instructed in the languages. The learning of

Greek and Latin, I am told, is going into disuse in Europe. I know not what their manners and occupations may call for: but it would be very ill-judged in us to follow their example in this instance. There is a certain period of life, say from eight to sixteen years of age, when the mind, like the body, is not yet firm enough for laborious and close operations. If applied to such, it falls an early victim to premature exertion; exhibiting indeed at first, in these young and tender subjects, the flattering appearance of their being men while they are yet children, but ending in reducing them to be children when they should be men. The memory is then most susceptible and tenacious of impressions; and the learning of languages being chiefly a work of memory, it seems precisely fitted to the powers of this period, which is long enough too for acquiring the most useful languages antient and modern. I do not pretend that language is science. It is only an instrument for the attainment of science. But that time is not lost which is employed in providing tools for future operation: more especially as in this case the books put into the hands of the youth for this purpose may be such as will at the same time impress their minds with useful facts and good principles. If this period be suffered to pass in idleness, the mind becomes lethargic and impotent, as would the body it inhabits if unexercised during the same time. The sympathy between body and mind during their rise, progress and decline, is too strict and obvious to endanger our being misled while we reason from the one to the other.—As soon as they are of sufficient age, it is supposed they will be sent on from the grammar schools to the university, which constitutes our third and last stage, there to study those sciences which may be adapted to their views.—By that part of our plan which prescribes the selection of the youths of genius from among the classes of the poor, we hope to avail the state of those talents which nature has sown as liberally among the poor as the rich, but which perish without use, if not sought for and cultivated.—But of all the views of this law none is more important, none more legitimate, than that of rendering the people the safe, as they are the ultimate, guardians of their own liberty. For this purpose the reading in the first stage, where *they* will receive their whole education, is proposed, as has been said, to be chiefly historical. History by apprising them of the past will enable them to judge of the future; it will avail them of the experience of other times and other nations; it will qualify them as judges of the actions and designs of men; it will enable them to know ambition under every disguise it may assume; and knowing it, to defeat its views. In every government on earth is some trace of human weakness, some germ of corruption and degeneracy, which cunning will discover, and wickedness insensibly open, cultivate, and improve. Every government degenerates when trusted to the rulers of the people alone. The people themselves therefore are its only safe depositories. And to render even them safe their minds must be improved to a certain degree. This indeed is not all that is necessary, though it be essentially necessary. An amendment of our constitution must here come in aid of the public education. The influence over government must be shared among all the people. If every individual which composes their mass participates of the ultimate authority, the government will be safe; because the corrupting the whole mass will exceed any private resources of wealth: and public ones cannot be provided but by levies on the people. In this case every man would have to pay his own price. The government of Great-Britain has been corrupted, because but one man in ten has a right to vote for members of parliament. The sellers of the government therefore get nine-tenths of their price clear. It has been thought that corruption is restrained by confining the right of suffrage to a few of the wealthier of the people: but it would be more effectually restrained by an extension of that right to such numbers as would bid defiance to the means of corruption. . . .

Query XVII: Religion

. . . The present state of our laws on the subject of religion is this. The convention of May 1776,[24] in their declaration of rights, declared it to be a truth, and a natural right, that the exercise of religion should be free; but when they proceeded to form on that declaration the ordinance of government, instead of taking up every principle declared in the bill of rights, and guarding it by legislative sanction, they passed

[24]The Virginia constitutional convention of 1776; Jefferson refers to Article 16 of the Virginia Declaration of Rights.—*Editor*

over that which asserted our religious rights, leaving them as they found them. The same convention, however, when they met as a member of the general assembly in October 1776, repealed all *acts of parliament* which had rendered criminal the maintaining any opinions in matters of religion, the forbearing to repair to church, and the exercising any mode of worship; and suspended the laws giving salaries to the clergy, which suspension was made perpetual in October 1779. Statutory oppressions in religion being thus wiped away, we remain at present under those only imposed by the common law, or by our own acts of assembly. At the common law, *heresy* was a capital offence, punishable by burning. Its definition was left to the ecclesiastical judges, before whom the conviction was, till the statute of the 1 El. c. 1. circumscribed it, by declaring, that nothing should be deemed heresy, but what had been so determined by authority of the canonical scriptures, or by one of the four first general councils, or by some other council having for the grounds of their declaration the express and plain words of the scriptures. Heresy, thus circumscribed, being an offence at the common law, our act of assembly of October 1777, c. 17 gives cognizance of it to the general court, by declaring, that the jurisdiction of that court shall be general in all matters at the common law. The execution is by the writ *De Haeretico comburendo.*[25] By our own act of assembly of 1705, c. 30, if a person brought up in the Christian religion denies the being of a God, or the Trinity, or asserts there are more Gods than one, or denies the Christian religion to be true, or the scriptures to be of divine authority, he is punishable on the first offence by incapacity to hold any office or employment ecclesiastical, civil, or military; on the second by disability to sue, to take any gift or legacy, to be guardian, executor, or administrator, and by three years imprisonment, without bail. A father's right to the custody of his own children being founded in law on his right of guardianship, this being taken away, they may of course be severed from him, and put, by the authority of a court, into more orthodox hands. This is a summary view of that religious slavery, under which a people have been willing to remain, who have lavished their lives and fortunes for the establishment of their civil freedom.

[25]"On burning a heretic."—*Editor*

The error seems not sufficiently eradicated, that the operations of the mind, as well as the acts of the body, are subject to the coercion of the laws. But our rulers can have authority over such natural rights only as we have submitted to them. The rights of conscience we never submitted, we could not submit. We are answerable for them to our God. The legitimate powers of government extend to such acts only as are injurious to others. But it does me no injury for my neighbour to say there are twenty gods, or no god. It neither picks my pocket nor breaks my leg. If it be said, his testimony in a court of justice cannot be relied on, reject it then, and be the stigma on him. Constraint may make him worse by making him a hypocrite, but it will never make him a truer man. It may fix him obstinately in his errors, but will not cure them. Reason and free enquiry are the only effectual agents against error. Give a loose to them, they will support the true religion, by bringing every false one to their tribunal, to the test of their investigation. They are the natural enemies of error, and of error only. Had not the Roman government permitted free enquiry, Christianity could never have been introduced. Had not free enquiry been indulged, at the era of the reformation, the corruptions of Christianity could not have been purged away. If it be restrained now, the present corruptions will be protected, and new ones encouraged. Was the government to prescribe to us our medicine and diet, our bodies would be in such keeping as our souls are now. Thus in France the emetic was once forbidden as a medicine, and the potatoe as an article of food. Government is just as infallible too when it fixes systems in physics. Galileo was sent to the inquisition for affirming that the earth was a sphere: the government had declared it to be as flat as a trencher, and Galileo was obliged to abjure his error. This error however at length prevailed, the earth became a globe, and Descartes declared it was whirled round its axis by a vortex. The government in which he lived was wise enough to see that this was no question of civil jurisdiction, or we should all have been involved by authority in vortices. In fact, the vortices have been exploded, and the Newtonian principle of gravitation is now more firmly established, on the basis of reason, than it would be were the government to step in, and to make it an article of necessary faith. Reason and experiment have been indulged, and error has fled before them. It is error alone which needs the support of government. Truth can stand by itself. Subject opinion to coercion: whom will you make your inquisitors? Fallible men; men governed by bad passions, by private as well as public reasons. And why subject it to coercion? To produce uniformity. But is uniformity of opinion desireable? No more than of face and stature. Introduce the bed of Procrustes then, and as there is danger that the large men may beat the small, make us all of a size, by lopping the former and stretching the latter. Difference of opinion is advantageous in religion. The several sects perform the office of a *Censor morum*[26] over each other. Is uniformity attainable? Millions of innocent men, women, and children, since the introduction of Christianity, have been burnt, tortured, fined, imprisoned; yet we have not advanced one inch towards uniformity. What has been the effect of coercion? To make one half the world fools, and the other half hypocrites. To support roguery and error all over the earth. Let us reflect that it is inhabited by a thousand millions of people. That these profess probably a thousand different systems of religion. That ours is but one of that thousand. That if there be but one right, and ours that one, we should wish to see the 999 wandering sects gathered into the fold of truth. But against such a majority we cannot effect this by force. Reason and persuasion are the only practicable instruments. To make way for these, free enquiry must be indulged; and how can we wish others to indulge it while we refuse it ourselves. But every state, says an inquisitor, has established some religion. No two, say I, have established the same. Is this a proof of the infallibility of establishments? Our sister states of Pennsylvania and New York, however, have long subsisted without any establishment at all. The experiment was new and doubtful when they made it. It has answered beyond conception. They flourish infinitely. Religion is well supported; of various kinds, indeed, but all good enough; all sufficient to preserve peace and order: or if a sect arises, whose tenets would subvert morals, good sense has fair play, and reasons and laughs it out of doors, without suffering the state to be troubled with it. They do not hang more malefactors than we do. They are not more disturbed with religious

[26]"Censor of morals"—*Editor*

dissensions. On the contrary, their harmony is unparalleled, and can be ascribed to nothing but their unbounded tolerance, because there is no other circumstance in which they differ from every nation on earth. They have made the happy discovery, that the way to silence religious disputes, is to take no notice of them. Let us too give this experiment fair play, and get rid, while we may, of those tyrannical laws. It is true, we are as yet secured against them by the spirit of the times. I doubt whether the people of this country would suffer an execution for heresy, or a three years imprisonment for not comprehending the mysteries of the Trinity. But is the spirit of the people an infallible, a permanent reliance? Is it government? Is this the kind of protection we receive in return for the rights we give up? Besides, the spirit of the times may alter, will alter. Our rulers will become corrupt, our people careless. A single zealot may commence persecutor, and better men be his victims. It can never be too often repeated, that the time for fixing every essential right on a legal basis is while our rulers are honest, and ourselves united. From the conclusion of this war we shall be going down hill. It will not then be necessary to resort every moment to the people for support. They will be forgotten, therefore, and their rights disregarded. They will forget themselves, but in the sole faculty of making money, and will never think of uniting to effect a due respect for their rights. The shackles, therefore, which shall not be knocked off at the conclusion of this war, will remain on us long, will be made heavier and heavier, till our rights shall revive or expire in a convulsion.

Query XVIII: Manners

It is difficult to determine on the standard by which the manners of a nation may be tried, whether *catholic,* or *particular.* It is more difficult for a native to bring to that standard the manners of his own nation, familiarized to him by habit. There must doubtless be an unhappy influence on the manners of our people produced by the existence of slavery among us. The whole commerce between master and slave is a perpetual exercise of the most boisterous passions, the most unremitting despotism on the one part, and degrading submissions on the other. Our children see this, and learn to imitate it; for man is an imitative animal. This quality is the germ of all education in him. From his cradle to his grave he is learning to do what he sees others do. If a parent could find no motive either in his philanthropy or his self-love, for restraining the intemperance of passion towards his slave, it should always be a sufficient one that his child is present. But generally it is not sufficient. The parent storms, the child looks on, catches the lineaments of wrath, puts on the same airs in the circle of smaller slaves, gives a loose to his worst of passions, and thus nursed, educated, and daily exercised in tyranny, cannot but be stamped by it with odious peculiarities. The man must be a prodigy who can retain his manners and morals undepraved by such circumstances. And with what execration should the statesman be loaded, who permitting one half the citizens thus to trample on the rights of the other, transforms those into despots, and these into enemies, destroys the morals of the one part, and the amor patriae of the other. For if a slave can have a country in this world, it must be any other in preference to that in which he is born to live and labour for another: in which he must lock up the faculties of his nature, contribute as far as depends on his individual endeavours to the evanishment of the human race, or entail his own miserable condition on the endless generations proceeding from him. With the morals of the people, their industry also is destroyed. For in a warm climate, no man will labour for himself who can make another labour for him. This is so true, that of the proprietors of slaves a very small proportion indeed are ever seen to labour. And can the liberties of a nation be thought secure when we have removed their only firm basis, a conviction in the minds of the people that these liberties are of the gift of God? That they are not to be violated but with his wrath? Indeed I tremble for my country when I reflect that God is just: that his justice cannot sleep for ever: that considering numbers, nature and natural means only, a revolution of the wheel of fortune, an exchange of situation, is among possible events: that it may become probable by supernatural interference! The Almighty has no attribute which can take side with us in such a contest.—But it is impossible to be temperate and to pursue this subject through the various considerations of policy, of morals, of history natural and civil. We must be contented to hope they will force their way into every one's mind. I think a change already perceptible,

since the origin of the present revolution. The spirit of the
master is abating, that of the slave rising from the dust, his
condition mollifying, the way I hope preparing, under the
auspices of heaven, for a total emancipation, and that this is
disposed, in the order of events, to be with the consent of
the masters, rather than by their extirpation.

Query XIX: Manufactures

. . . The political economists of Europe have established it
as a principle that every state should endeavour to manufacture for itself: and this principle, like many others, we transfer to America, without calculating the difference of
circumstance which should often produce a difference of
result. In Europe the lands are either cultivated, or locked
up against the cultivator. Manufacture must therefore be
resorted to of necessity not of choice, to support the surplus
of their people. But we have an immensity of land courting
the industry of the husbandman. Is it best then that all our
citizens should be employed in its improvement, or that one
half should be called off from that to exercise manufactures
and handicraft arts for the other? Those who labour in the
earth are the chosen people of God, if ever he had a chosen
people, whose breasts he has made his peculiar deposit for
substantial and genuine virtue. It is the focus in which he
keeps alive that sacred fire, which otherwise might escape
from the face of the earth. Corruption of morals in the mass
of cultivators is a phenomenon of which no age nor nation
has furnished an example. It is the mark set on those, who
not looking up to heaven, to their own soil and industry, as
does the husbandman, for their subsistance, depend for it
on the casualties and caprice of customers. Dependance begets subservience and venality, suffocates the germ of virtue,
and prepares fit tools for the designs of ambition. This, the
natural progress and consequence of the arts, has sometimes perhaps been retarded by accidental circumstances:
but, generally speaking, the proportion which the aggregate
of the other classes of citizens bears in any state to that of

its husbandmen, is the proportion of its unsound to its healthy parts, and is a good-enough barometer whereby to measure its degree of corruption. While we have land to labour then, let us never wish to see our citizens occupied at a work-bench, or twirling a distaff. Carpenters, masons, smiths, are wanting in husbandry: but, for the general operations of manufacture, let our work-shops remain in Europe. It is better to carry provisions and materials to workmen there, than bring them to the provisions and materials, and with them their manners and principles. The loss by the transportation of commodities across the Atlantic will be made up in happiness and permanence of government. The mobs of great cities add just so much to the support of pure government, as sores do to the strength of the human body. It is the manners and spirit of a people which preserve a republic in vigour. A degeneracy in these is a canker which soon eats to the heart of its laws and constitution.

Query XXII: Public Revenue and Expenses[27]

. . . To this estimate of our abilities, let me add a word as to the application of them, if, when cleared of the present contest, and of the debts with which that will charge us, we come to measure force hereafter with any European power. Such events are devoutly to be deprecated. Young as we are, and with such a country before us to fill with people and with happiness, we should point in that direction the whole generative force of nature, wasting none of it in efforts of mutual destruction. It should be our endeavour to cultivate the peace and friendship of every nation, even of that which has injured us most, when we shall have carried our point against her. Our interest will be to throw open the doors of commerce, and to knock off all its shackles, giving perfect freedom to all persons for the vent of whatever they may chuse to bring into our ports, and asking the same in theirs. Never was so much false arithmetic employed on any sub-

[27]Jefferson favors a peaceful policy for independent America, but he stops short of advocating pacifism and proposes a small navy. —*Editor*

ject, as that which has been employed to persuade nations that it is their interest to go to war. Were the money which it has cost to gain, at the close of a long war, a little town, or a little territory, the right to cut wood here, or to catch fish there, expended in improving what they already possess, in making roads, opening rivers, building ports, improving the arts, and finding employment for their idle poor, it would render them much stronger, much wealthier and happier. This I hope will be our wisdom. And, perhaps, to remove as much as possible the occasions of making war, it might be better for us to abandon the ocean altogether, that being the element whereon we shall be principally exposed to jostle with other nations: to leave to others to bring what we shall want, and to carry what we can spare. This would make us invulnerable to Europe, by offering none of our property to their prize, and would turn all our citizens to the cultivation of the earth; and, I repeat it again, cultivators of the earth are the most virtuous and independent citizens. It might be time enough to seek employment for them at sea, when the land no longer offers it. But the actual habits of our countrymen attach them to commerce. They will exercise it for themselves. Wars then must sometimes be our lot; and all the wise can do, will be to avoid that half of them which would be produced by our own follies, and our own acts of injustice; and to make for the other half the best preparations we can. Of what nature should these be? A land army would be useless for offence, and not the best nor safest instrument of defence. For either of these purposes, the sea is the field on which we should meet an European enemy. On that element it is necessary we should possess some power. To aim at such a navy as the greater nations of Europe possess, would be a foolish and wicked waste of the energies of our countrymen. It would be to pull on our own heads that load of military expence, which makes the European labourer go supperless to bed, and moistens his bread with the sweat of his brows. It will be enough if we enable ourselves to prevent insults from those nations of Europe which are weak on the sea, because circumstances exist, which render even the stronger ones weak as to us. Providence has placed their richest and most defenceless possessions at our door; has obliged their most precious commerce to pass as it were in review before us. To protect

this, or to assail us, a small part only of their naval force will
ever be risqued across the Atlantic. The dangers to which
the elements expose them here are too well known, and the
greater dangers to which they would be exposed at home,
were any general calamity to involve their whole fleet. They
can attack us by detachment only; and it will suffice to make
ourselves equal to what they may detach. Even a smaller
force than they may detach will be rendered equal or superior by the quickness with which any check may be repaired
with us, while losses with them will be irreparable till too
late. A small naval force then is sufficient for us, and a small
one is necessary. . . .

Draft of the Kentucky
Resolutions[1]

NOVEMBER, 1798

1. *Resolved,* That the several States composing the United
States of America, are not united on the principle of unlimited submission to their general government; but that, by a
compact under the style and title of a Constitution for the
United States, and of amendments thereto, they constituted
a general government for special purposes—delegated to
that government certain definite powers, reserving, each
State to itself, the residuary mass of right to their own self-
government; and that whensoever the general government
assumes undelegated powers, its acts are unauthoritative,
void and of no force: that to this compact each State acceded
as a State, and is an integral party, its co-States forming, as
to itself, the other party: that the government created by this
compact was not made the exclusive or final judge of the
extent of the powers delegated to itself; since that would

[1]These resolutions were adopted by the Kentucky legislature to
protest the Alien and Sedition laws. Jefferson kept his authorship
a secret until 1821. The Kentucky resolutions should be compared
with the Virginia resolutions authored by Madison.—*Editor*

have made its discretion, and not the Constitution, the measure of its powers; but that, as in all other cases of compact among powers having no common judge, each party has an equal right to judge for itself, as well of infractions as of the mode and measure of redress.

2. *Resolved,* That the Constitution of the United States, having delegated to Congress a power to punish treason, counterfeiting the securities and current coin of the United States, piracies, and felonies committed on the high seas, and offences against the law of nations, and no other crimes whatsoever; and it being true as a general principle, and one of the amendments to the Constitution having also declared, that "the powers not delegated to the United States by the Constitution, nor prohibited by it to the States, are reserved to the States respectively, or to the people," therefore the act of Congress, passed on the 14th day of July, 1798, and intituled "An Act in addition to the act intituled An Act for the punishment of certain crimes against the United States," as also the act passed by them on the ____ day of June, 1798, intituled "An Act to punish frauds committed on the bank of the United States," (and all their other acts which assume to create, define, or punish crimes, other than those so enumerated in the Constitution,) are altogether void, and of no force; and that the power to create, define, and punish such other crimes is reserved, and, of right, appertains solely and exclusively to the respective States, each within its own territory.

3. *Resolved,* That it is true as a general principle, and is also expressly declared by one of the amendments to the Constitution, that "the powers not delegated to the United States by the Constitution, nor prohibited by it to the States, are reserved to the States respectively, or to the people"; and that no power over the freedom of religion, freedom of speech, or freedom of the press being delegated to the United States by the Constitution, nor prohibited by it to the States, all lawful powers respecting the same did of right remain, and were reserved to the States or the people: that thus was manifested their determination to retain to themselves the right of judging how far the licentiousness of speech and of the press may be abridged without lessening their useful freedom, and how far those abuses which cannot be separated from their use should be tolerated, rather than

the use be destroyed. And thus also they guarded against all abridgment by the United States of the freedom of religious opinions and exercises, and retained to themselves the right of protecting the same, as this State, by a law passed on the general demand of its citizens, had already protected them from all human restraint or interference. And that in addition to this general principle and express declaration, another and more special provision has been made by one of the amendments to the Constitution, which expressly declares, that "Congress shall make no law respecting an establishment of religion, or prohibiting the free exercise thereof, or abridging the freedom of speech or of the press": thereby guarding in the same sentence, and under the same words, the freedom of religion, of speech, and of the press: insomuch, that whatever violated either, throws down the sanctuary which covers the others, and that libels, falsehood, and defamation, equally with heresy and false religion, are withheld from the cognizance of federal tribunals. That, therefore, the act of Congress of the United States, passed on the 14th day of July, 1798, intituled "An Act in addition to the act intituled An Act for the punishment of certain crimes against the United States," which does abridge the freedom of the press, is not law, but is altogether void, and of no force.

4. *Resolved,* That alien friends are under the jurisdiction and protection of the laws of the State wherein they are: that no power over them has been delegated to the United States, nor prohibited to the individual States, distinct from their power over citizens. And it being true as a general principle, and one of the amendments to the Constitution having also declared, that "the powers not delegated to the United States by the Constitution, nor prohibited by it to the States, are reserved to the States respectively, or to the people," the act of the Congress of the United States, passed on the _____ day of July, 1798, intituled "An Act concerning aliens," which assumes power over alien friends, not delegated by the Constitution, is not law, but is altogether void, and of no force.

5. *Resolved,* That in addition to the general principle, as well as the express declaration, that powers not delegated are reserved, another and more special provision, inserted in the Constitution from abundant caution, has declared

that "the migration or importation of such persons as any of the States now existing shall think proper to admit, shall not be prohibited by the Congress prior to the year 1808": that this commonwealth does admit the migration of alien friends, described as the subject of the said act concerning aliens: that a provision against prohibiting their migration, is a provision against all acts equivalent thereto, or it would be nugatory: that to remove them when migrated, is equivalent to a prohibition of their migration, and is, therefore, contrary to the said provision of the Constitution, and void.

6. *Resolved,* That the imprisonment of a person under the protection of the laws of this commonwealth, on his failure to obey the simple *order* of the President to depart out of the United States, as is undertaken by said act intituled "An Act concerning aliens," is contrary to the Constitution, one amendment to which has provided that "no person shall be deprived of liberty without due process of law"; and that another having provided that "in all criminal prosecutions the accused shall enjoy the right to public trial by an impartial jury, to be informed of the nature and cause of the accusation, to be confronted with the witnesses against him, to have compulsory process for obtaining witnesses in his favor, and to have the assistance of counsel for his defence," the same act, undertaking to authorize the President to remove a person out of the United States, who is under the protection of the law, on his own suspicion, without accusation, without jury, without public trial, without confrontation of the witnesses against him, without hearing witnesses in his favor, without defence, without counsel, is contrary to the provision also of the Constitution, is therefore not law, but utterly void, and of no force: that transferring the power of judging any person, who is under the protection of the laws, from the courts to the President of the United States, as is undertaken by the same act concerning aliens, is against the article of the Constitution which provides that "the judicial power of the United States shall be vested in courts, the judges of which shall hold their offices during good behavior"; and that the said act is void for that reason also. And it is further to be noted, that this transfer of judiciary power is to that magistrate of the general government who already possesses all the Executive, and a negative on all Legislative powers.

7. *Resolved,* That the construction applied by the General Government (as is evidenced by sundry of their proceedings) to those parts of the Constitution of the United States which delegate to Congress a power "to lay and collect taxes, duties, imports, and excises, to pay the debts, and provide for the common defence and general welfare of the United States," and "to make all laws which shall be necessary and proper for carrying into execution the powers vested by the Constitution in the government of the United States, or in any department or officer thereof," goes to the destruction of all limits prescribed to their power by the Constitution: that words meant by the instrument to be subsidiary only to the execution of limited powers, ought not to be so construed as themselves to give unlimited powers, nor a part to be so taken as to destroy the whole residue of that instrument: that the proceedings of the General Government under color of these articles, will be a fit and necessary subject of revisal and correction, at a time of greater tranquillity, while those specified in the preceding resolutions call for immediate redress.

8. *Resolved,* That a committee of conference and correspondence be appointed, who shall have in charge to communicate the preceding resolutions to the Legislatures of the several States; to assure them that this commonwealth continues in the same esteem of their friendship and union which it has manifested from that moment at which a common danger first suggested a common union: that it considers union, for specified national purposes, and particularly to those specified in their late federal compacts, to be friendly to the peace, happiness and prosperity of all the States: that faithful to that compact, according to the plain intent and meaning in which it was understood and acceded to by the several parties, it is sincerely anxious for its preservation: that it does also believe, that to take from the States all the powers of self-government and transfer them to a general and consolidated government, without regard to the special delegations and reservations solemnly agreed to in that compact, is not for the peace, happiness or prosperity of these States; and that therefore this commonwealth is determined, as it doubts not its co-States are, to submit to undelegated, and consequently unlimited powers in no man, or body of men on earth: that in cases of an abuse of the

delegated powers, the members of the general government, being chosen by the people, a change by the people would be the constitutional remedy; but, where powers are assumed which have not been delegated, a nullification of the act is the rightful remedy: that every State has a natural right in cases not within the compact, (*casus non fœderis,*) to nullify of their own authority all assumptions of power by others within their limits: that without this right, they would be under the dominion, absolute and unlimited, of whosoever might exercise this right of judgment for them: that nevertheless, this commonwealth, from motives of regard and respect for its co-States, has wished to communicate with them on the subject: that with them alone it is proper to communicate, they alone being parties to the compact, and solely authorized to judge in the last resort of the powers exercised under it, Congress being not a party, but merely the creature of the compact, and subject as to its assumptions of power to the final judgment of those by whom, and for whose use itself and its powers were all created and modified: that if the acts before specified should stand, these conclusions would flow from them; that the general government may place any act they think proper on the list of crimes, and punish it themselves whether enumerated or not enumerated by the constitution as cognizable by them: that they may transfer its cognizance to the President, or any other person, who may himself be the accuser, counsel, judge and jury, whose *suspicions* may be the evidence, his *order* the sentence, his *officer* the executioner, and his breast the sole record of the transaction: that a very numerous and valuable description of the inhabitants of these States being, by this precedent, reduced, as outlaws, to the absolute dominion of one man, and the barrier of the Constitution thus swept away from us all, no rampart now remains against the passions and the powers of a majority in Congress to protect from a like exportation, or other more grievous punishment, the minority of the same body, the legislatures, judges, governors and counsellors of the States, nor their other peaceable inhabitants, who may venture to reclaim the constitutional rights and liberties of the States and people, or who for other causes, good or bad, may be obnoxious to the views, or marked by the suspicions of the President, or be thought dangerous to his or their election, or other interests, public or personal: that the friendless alien has indeed been selected as the safest subject of a first experiment; but the citizen will soon follow, or rather, has already followed, for already has a sedition act marked him as its prey: that these and successive acts of the same character, unless arrested at the threshold, necessarily drive these States into revolution and blood, and will furnish new calumnies against republican government, and new pretexts for those who wish it to be believed that man cannot be governed but by a rod of iron: that it would be a dangerous delusion were a confidence in the men of our choice to silence our fears for the safety of our rights: that confidence is everywhere the parent of despotism—free government is founded in jealousy, and not in confidence; it is jealousy and not confidence which prescribes limited constitutions, to bind down those whom we are obliged to trust with power: that our Constitution has accordingly fixed the limits to which, and no further, our confidence may go; and let the honest advocate of confidence read the Alien and Sedition acts, and say if the Constitution has not been wise in fixing limits to the government it created, and whether we should be wise in destroying those limits. Let him say what the government is, if it be not a tyranny, which the men of our choice have conferred on our President, and the President of our choice has assented to, and accepted over the friendly strangers to whom the mild spirit of our country and its laws have pledged hospitality and protection: that the men of our choice have more respected the bare *suspicions* of the President, than the solid right of innocence, the claims of justification, the sacred force of truth, and the forms and substance of law and justice. In questions of power, then, let no more be heard of confidence in man, but bind him down from mischief by the chains of the Constitution. That this commonwealth does therefore call on its co-States for an expression of their sentiments on the acts concerning aliens, and for the punishment of certain crimes herein before specified, plainly declaring whether these acts are or are not authorized by the federal compact, And it doubts not that their sense will be so announced as to prove their attachment unaltered to limited government, whether general or particular. And that the rights and liberties of their co-States will be exposed to no dangers by remaining embarked in a common bottom with their own. That they will concur with this common-wealth in considering the said acts as so palpably against the Constitution as to amount to an undisguised declaration that that compact is not meant to be the measure of the powers of the General Government, but that it will proceed in the exercise over these States, of all powers whatsoever: that they will view this as seizing the rights of the States, and consolidating them in the hands of the General Govern-ment, with a power assumed to bind the States (not merely as the cases made federal, *casus fœderis* but), in all cases whatsoever, by laws made, not with their consent, but by others against their consent: that this would be to surrender the form of government we have chosen, and live under one deriving its powers from its own will, and not from our authority; and that the co-States, recurring to their natural right in cases not made federal, will concur in declaring these acts void, and of no force, and will each take measures of its own for providing that neither these acts, nor any others of the General Government not plainly and intention-ally authorized by the Constitution, shall be exercised within their respective territories.

9. *Resolved,* That the said committee be authorized to communicate by writing or personal conferences, at any times or places whatever, with any person or persons who may be appointed by any one or more co-States to corre-spond or confer with them; and that they lay their proceed-ings before the next session of Assembly.

First Inaugural Address

MARCH 4, 1801

Friends and Fellow Citizens:

Called upon to undertake the duties of the first executive office of our country, I avail myself of the presence of that portion of my fellow citizens which is here assembled, to express my grateful thanks for the favor with which they have been pleased to look toward me, to declare a sincere approach it with those anxious and awful presentiments which the greatness of the charge and the weakness of my powers so justly inspire. A rising nation, spread over a wise and fruitful land, traversing all the seas with the rich productions of their industry, engaged in commerce with nations who feel power and forget right, advancing rapidly to destinies beyond the reach of mortal eye—when I contemplate these transcendent objects, and see the honor, the happiness, and the hopes of this beloved country committed to the issue and the auspices of this day, I shrink from the contemplation, and humble myself before the magnitude of the undertaking. Utterly indeed, should I despair, did not the presence of many whom I here see remind me, that in the other high authorities provided by our constitution, I shall find resources of wisdom, of virtue, and of zeal, on which to rely under all difficulties. To you, then, gentlemen, who are charged with the sovereign functions of legislation, and to those associated with you, I look with encouragement for that guidance and support which may enable us to steer with safety the vessel in which we are all embarked amid the conflicting elements of a troubled world.

During the contest of opinion through which we have passed, the animation of discussion and of exertions has sometimes worn an aspect which might impose on strangers unused to think freely and to speak and to write what they think; but this being now decided by the voice of the nation, announced according to the rules of the constitution, all will, of course, arrange themselves under the will of the law, and unite in common efforts for the common good. All, too, will bear in mind this sacred principle, that though the will of the majority is in all cases to prevail, that will, to be rightful, must be reasonable; that the minority possess their equal rights, which equal laws must protect, and to violate which would be oppression. Let us, then, fellow citizens, unite with one heart and one mind. Let us restore to social intercourse that harmony and affection without which liberty and even life itself are but dreary things. And let us reflect that having banished from our land that religious intolerance under which mankind so long bled and suffered, we have yet gained little if we countenance a political intolerance as despotic, as wicked, and capable of as bitter and bloody persecutions. During the throes and convulsions of the ancient world, during the agonizing spasms of infuriated man, seeking through blood and slaughter his long-lost liberty, it was not wonderful that the agitations of the billows should reach even this distant and peaceful shore; that this should be more felt and feared by some and less by others; that this should divide opinions as to measures of safety. But every difference of opinion is not a difference of principle. We have called by different names brethren of the same principle. We are all republicans—we are federalists. If there be any among us who would wish to dissolve this Union or to change its republican form, let them stand undisturbed as monuments of the safety with which error of opinion may be tolerated where reason is left free to combat it. I know, indeed, that some honest men fear that a republican government cannot be strong; that this government is not strong enough. But would the honest patriot, in the full tide of successful experiment, abandon a government which has so far kept us free and firm, on the theoretic and visionary fear that this government, the world's best hope, may by possibility want energy to preserve itself? I trust not. I believe this, on the contrary, the strongest government on earth. I believe it is the only one where every man, at the call of the laws, would fly to the standard of the law, and would meet invasions of the public order as his own personal concern. Sometimes it is said that man cannot be trusted with the government of himself. Can he, then, be trusted with the government of others? Or have we found angels in the forms of kings to govern him? Let history answer this question.

Let us, then, with courage and confidence pursue our own federal and republican principles, our attachment to our union and representative government. Kindly separated by nature and a wide ocean from the exterminating havoc of one quarter of the globe; too high-minded to endure the degradations of the others; possessing a chosen country, with room enough for our descendants to the hundredth and thousandth generation; entertaining a due sense of our equal right to the use of our own faculties, to the acquisitions of our industry, to honor and confidence from our fellow citizens, resulting not from birth but from our actions and their sense of them; enlightened by a benign religion, professed, indeed, and practiced in various forms, yet all of them including honesty, truth, temperance, gratitude, and the love of man; acknowledging and adoring an overruling Providence, which by all its dispensations proves that it delights in the happiness of man here and his greater happiness hereafter; with all these blessings, what more is necessary to make us a happy and prosperous people? Still one thing more, fellow citizens—a wise and frugal government, which shall restrain men from injuring one another, which shall leave them otherwise free to regulate their own pursuits of industry and improvement, and shall not take from the mouth of labor the bread it has earned. This is the sum of good government, and this is necessary to close the circle of our felicities.

About to enter, fellow citizens, on the exercise of duties which comprehend everything dear and valuable to you, it is proper that you should understand what I deem the essential principles of our government, and consequently those which ought to shape its administration. I will compress them within the narrowest compass they will bear, stating the general principle, but not all its limitations. Equal and exact justice to all men, of whatever state or persuasion, religious or political; peace, commerce, and honest friendship, with all nations—entangling alliances with none; the support of the state governments in all their rights, as the most competent administrations for our domestic concerns and the surest bulwarks against antirepublican tendencies; the preservation of the general government in its whole constitutional vigor, as the sheet anchor of our peace at home and safety abroad; a jealous care of the right of election by the people—a mild and safe corrective of abuses which are lopped by the sword of the revolution where peaceable remedies are unprovided; absolute acquiescence in the decisions of the majority—the vital principle of republics, from which there is no appeal but to force, the vital principle and immediate parent of despotism; a well-disciplined militia—our best reliance in peace and for the first moments of war, till regulars may relieve them; the supremacy of the civil over the military authority; economy in the public expense, that labor may be lightly burdened; the honest payment of our debts and sacred preservation of the public faith; encouragement of agriculture, and of commerce as its handmaid; the diffusion of information and the arraignment of all abuses at the bar of public reason; freedom of religion; freedom of the press; freedom of person under the protection of the habeas corpus; and trial by juries impartially selected—these principles form the bright constellation which has gone before us, and guided our steps through an age of revolution and reformation. The wisdom of our sages and the blood of our heroes have been devoted to their attainment. They should be the creed of our political faith—the text of civil instruction—the touchstone by which to try the services of those we trust; and should we wander from them in moments of error or alarm, let us hasten to retrace our steps and to regain the road which alone leads to peace, liberty, and safety.

I repair, then, fellow citizens, to the post you have assigned me. With experience enough in subordinate offices to have seen the difficulties of this, the greatest of all, I have learned to expect that it will rarely fall to the lot of imperfect man to retire from this station with the reputation and the favor which bring him into it. Without pretensions to that high confidence reposed in our first and great revolutionary character, whose preeminent services had entitled him to the first place in his country's love, and destined for him the fairest page in the volume of faithful history, I ask so much confidence only as may give firmness and effect to the legal administration of your affairs. I shall often go wrong through defect of judgment. When right, I shall often be thought wrong by those whose positions will not command a view of the whole ground. I ask your indulgence for my own errors, which will never be intentional; and your support against the errors of others, who may condemn what they would not if seen in all its parts. The approbation implied by your suffrage is a consolation to me for the past; and my future solicitude will be to retain the good opinion of those who have bestowed it in advance, to conciliate that of others by doing them all the good in my power, and to be instrumental to the happiness and freedom of all.

Relying, then, on the patronage of your good will, I advance with obedience to the work, ready to retire from it whenever you become sensible how much better choice it is in your power to make. And may that Infinite Power which rules the destinies of the universe, lead our councils to what is best, and give them a favorable issue for your peace and prosperity.

A Selection of Letters

To James Madison, January 30, 1787

I am impatient to learn your sentiments on the late troubles in the eastern States.[1] So far as I have yet seen they do not appear to threaten serious consequences. Those States have suffered by the stoppage of the channels of their commerce, which have not yet found other issues. This must render money scarce and make the people uneasy. This uneasiness has produced acts absolutely unjustifiable, but I hope they will provoke no severities from their governments. A consciousness of those in power that their administration of the public affairs has been honest may, perhaps, produce too great a degree of indignation, and those characters wherein fear predominates over hope may apprehend too much from these instances of irregularity. They may conclude too hastily that nature has formed man insusceptible of any other government than that of force, a conclusion not founded in truth nor experience. Societies exist under three forms, sufficiently distinguishable: (1) without government, as among our Indians; (2) under governments wherein the will of everyone has a just influence, as is the case in England in a slight degree and in our States in a great one; (3) under governments of force, as is the case in all other monarchies and in most of the other republics. To have an idea of the curse of existence under these last, they must be seen. It is a government of wolves over sheep. It is a problem, not clear in my mind, that the first condition is not the best. But I believe it to be inconsistent with any great degree of population. The second state has a great deal of good in it. The mass of mankind under that enjoys a precious degree of liberty and happiness. It has its evils, too, the principal of which is the turbulence to which it is subject. But weigh this against the oppressions of monarchy and it becomes nothing. *Malo periculosam libertatem quam quietam ser-*

[1]The "late troubles" were Shays' rebellion, an uprising of debtors in western Massachusetts in 1786–1787.—*Editor*

vitutem[2] Even this evil is productive of good. It prevents the
degeneracy of government and nourishes a general attention to the public affairs. I hold it that a little rebellion now
and then is a good thing, and as necessary in the political
world as storms in the physical. Unsuccessful rebellions,
indeed, generally establish the encroachments on the rights
of the people which have produced them. An observation of
this truth should render honest republican governors so
mild in their punishment of rebellions as not to discourage
them too much. It is a medicine necessary for the sound
health of government.

To James Madison, December 20, 1787

I like much the general idea of framing a government,
which should go on of itself, peaceably, without needing
continual recurrence to the State legislatures. I like the organization of the government into legislative, judiciary and
executive. I like the power given the legislature to levy taxes,
and for that reason solely, I approve of the greater House
being chosen by the people directly. For though I think a
House so chosen, will be very far inferior to the present
Congress, will be very illy qualified to legislate for the
Union, for foreign nations, &c., yet this evil does not weigh
against the good, of preserving inviolate the fundamental
principle, that the people are not to be taxed but by representatives chosen immediately by themselves. I am cap-
tivated by the compromise of the opposite claims of the
great and little States, of the latter to equal, and the former
to proportional influence. I am much pleased too, with the
substitution of the method of voting by person, instead of
that of voting by States; and I like the negative given to the
Executive, conjointly with a third of either House; though I
should have liked it better, had the judiciary been associated
for that purpose, or invested separately with a similar power.
There are other good things of less moment. I will now tell
you what I do not like. First, the omission of a bill of rights,
providing clearly, and without the aid of sophism, for freedom of religion, freedom of the press, protection against
standing armies, restriction of monopolies, the eternal and

[2]"I prefer dangerous liberty to quiet servitude."—*Editor*

unremitting force of the habeas corpus laws, and trials by jury in all matters of fact triable by the laws of the land, and not by the laws of nations. To say, as Mr. Wilson does, that a bill of rights was not necessary, because all is reserved in the case of the general government which is not given, while in the particular ones, all is given which is not reserved, might do for the audience to which it was addressed; but it is surely a *gratis dictum,* the reverse of which might just as well be said; and it is opposed by strong inferences from the body of the instrument, as well as from the omission of the cause of our present Confederation, which had made the reservation in express terms. It was hard to conclude, because there has been a want of uniformity among the States as to the cases triable by jury, because some have been so incautious as to dispense with this mode of trial in certain cases, therefore, the more prudent States shall be reduced to the same level of calamity. It would have been much more just and wise to have concluded the other way, that as most of the States had preserved with jealousy this sacred palladium of liberty, those who had wandered, should be brought back to it; and to have established general right rather than general wrong. For I consider all the ill as established, which may be established. I have a right to nothing, which another has a right to take away; and Congress will have a right to take away trials by jury in all civil cases. Let me add, that a bill of rights is what the people are entitled to against every government on earth, general or particular; and what no just government should refuse, or rest on inference.

The second feature I dislike, and strongly dislike, is the abandonment, in every instance, of the principle of rotation in office, and most particularly in the case of the President. Reason and experience tell us, that the first magistrate will always be re-elected if he may be re-elected. He is then an officer for life. This once observed, it becomes of so much consequence to certain nations, to have a friend or a foe at the head of our affairs, that they will interfere with money and with arms. A Galloman, or an Angloman, will be supported by the nation he befriends. If once elected, and at a second or third election outvoted by one or two votes, he will pretend false votes, foul play, hold possession of the reins of government, be supported by the States voting for him, especially if they be the central ones, lying in a compact body themselves, and separating their opponents; and they will be aided by one nation in Europe, while the majority are aided by another. The election of a President of America, some years hence, will be much more interesting to certain nations of Europe, than ever the election of a King of Poland was. Reflect on all the instances in history, ancient and modern, of elective monarchies, and say if they do not give foundation for my fears; the Roman Emperors, the Popes while they were of any importance, the German Emperors till they became hereditary in practice, the Kings of Poland, the Deys of the Ottoman dependencies. It may be said, that if elections are to be attended with these disorders, the less frequently they are repeated the better. But experience says, that to free them from disorder, they must be rendered less interesting by a necessity of change. No foreign power, nor domestic party, will waste their blood and money to elect a person, who must go out at the end of a short period. The power of removing every fourth year by the vote of the people, is a power which they will not exercise, and if they were disposed to exercise it, they would not be permitted. The King of Poland is removable every day by the diet. But they never remove him. Nor would Russia, the Emperor, &c., permit them to do it. Smaller objections are, the appeals on matters of fact as well as laws; and the binding all persons, legislative, executive and judiciary by oath, to maintain that constitution. I do not pretend to decide, what would be the best method of procuring the establishment of the manifold good things in this constitution, and of getting rid of the bad. Whether by adopting it, in hopes of future amendment; or after it shall have been duly weighed and canvassed by the people, after seeing the parts they generally dislike, and those they generally approve, to say to them, "We see now what you wish. You are willing to give to your federal government such and such powers; but you wish, at the same time, to have such and such fundamental rights secured to you, and certain sources of convulsion taken away. Be it so. Send together deputies again. Let them establish your fundamental rights by a sacrosanct declaration, and let them pass the parts of the constitution you have approved. These will give powers to your federal government sufficient for your happiness."

This is what might be said, and would probably produce a speedy, more perfect and more permanent form of government. At all events, I hope you will not be discouraged from making other trials, if the present one should fail. We are never permitted to despair of the commonwealth. I have thus told you freely what I like, and what I dislike, merely as a matter of curiosity; for I know it is not in my power to offer matter of information to your judgment, which has been formed after hearing and weighing everything which the wisdom of man could offer on these subjects. I own, I am not a friend to a very energetic government. It is always oppressive. It places the governors indeed more at their ease, at the expense of the people. The late rebellion in Massachusetts has given more alarm, than I think it should have done. Calculate that one rebellion in thirteen States in the course of eleven years, is but one for each State in a century and a half. No country should be so long without one. Nor will any degree of power in the hands of government, prevent insurrections. In England, where the hand of power is heavier than with us, there are seldom half a dozen years without an insurrection. In France, where it is still heavier, but less despotic, as Montesquieu supposes, than in some other countries, and where there are always two or three hundred thousand men ready to crush insurrections, there have been three in the course of the three years I have been here, in every one of which greater numbers were engaged than in Massachusetts, and a great deal more blood was spilt. In Turkey, where the sole nod of the despot is death, insurrections are the events of every day. Compare again the ferocious depredations of their insurgents, with the order, the moderation and the almost self-extinguishment of ours. And say, finally, whether peace is best preserved by giving energy to the government, or information to the people. This last is the most certain, and the most legitimate engine of government. Educate and inform the whole mass of the people. Enable them to see that it is their interest to preserve peace and order, and they will preserve them. And it requires no very high degree of education to convince them of this. They are the only sure reliance for the preservation of our liberty. After all, it is my principle that the will of the majority should prevail. If they approve the proposed constitution in all its parts, I shall concur in it cheerfully, in hopes they will amend it, whenever they shall find it works wrong. This reliance cannot deceive us, as long as we remain virtuous; and I think we shall be so, as long as agriculture is our principal object, which will be the case, while there remains vacant lands in any part of America. When we get piled upon one another in large cities, as in Europe, we shall become corrupt as in Europe, and go to eating one another as they do there. I have tired you by this time with disquisitions which you have already heard repeated by others, a thousand and a thousand times; and therefore, shall only add assurances of the esteem and attachment with which I have the honor to be, dear Sir, your affectionate friend and servant.

To James Madison, March 15, 1789

In the arguments in favor of a declaration of rights, you omit one which has great weight with me; the legal check which it puts into the hands of the judiciary. This is a body, which, if rendered independent and kept strictly to their own department, merits great confidence for their learning and integrity. In fact, what degree of confidence would be too much, for a body composed of such men as Wythe, Blair and Pendleton?[3] On characters like these, the *"civium ardor prava jubentium"*[4] would make no impression. I am happy to find that, on the whole, you are a friend to this amendment. The declaration of rights is, like all other human blessings, alloyed with some inconveniences, and not accomplishing fully its object. But the good in this instance, vastly overweighs the evil. I cannot refrain from making short answers to the objections which your letter states to have been raised. 1. That the rights in question are reserved, by the manner in which the federal powers are granted. Answer. A

[3]George Wythe (1726–1806), John Blair (1732–1800), and Edmund Pendleton (1721–1803) were three distinguished Virginia jurists. Wythe was Jefferson's teacher of law; he and Pendleton served with Jefferson on the commission which proposed the "Revisal" of Virginia's laws in 1779. Blair was appointed to the U.S. Supreme Court in September 1789.—*Editor*
[4]"the perverse zeal of the ruling citizens."—*Editor*

constitutive act may, certainly, be so formed, as to need no declaration of rights. The act itself has the force of a declaration, as far as it goes; and if it goes to all material points, nothing more is wanting. In the draught of a constitution which I had once a thought of proposing in Virginia, and printed afterwards, I endeavored to reach all the great objects of public liberty, and did not mean to add a declaration of rights. Probably the object was imperfectly executed; but the deficiencies would have been supplied by others, in the course of discussion. But in a constitutive act which leaves some precious articles unnoticed, and raises implications against others, a declaration of rights becomes necessary, by way of supplement. This is the case of our new federal constitution. This instrument forms us into one State, as to certain objects, and gives us a legislative and executive body for these objects. It should, therefore, guard us against their abuses of power, within the field submitted to them. 2. A positive declaration of some essential rights could not be obtained in the requisite latitude. Answer. Half a loaf is better than no bread. If we cannot secure all our rights, let us secure what we can. 3. The limited powers of the federal government, and jealousy of the subordinate governments, afford a security which exists in no other instance. Answer. The first member of this seems resolvable into the first objection before stated. The jealousy of the subordinate governments is a precious reliance. But observe that those governments are only agents. They must have principles furnished them, whereon to found their opposition. The declaration of rights will be the text, whereby they will try all the acts of the federal government. In this view, it is necessary to the federal government also; as by the same text, they may try the opposition of the subordinate governments. 4. Experience proves the inefficacy of a bill of rights. True. But though it is not absolutely efficacious under all circumstances, it is of great potency always, and rarely inefficacious. A brace the more will often keep up the building which would have fallen, with that brace the less. There is a remarkable difference between the characters of the inconveniences which attend a declaration of rights, and those which attend the want of it. The inconveniences of the declaration are, that it may cramp government in its useful exertions. But the evil of this is short-lived, moderate and reparable. The inconveniences of the want of a declaration are permanent, afflicting and irreparable. They are in constant progression from bad to worse. The executive, in our governments, is not the sole, it is scarcely the principal object of my jealousy. The tyranny of the legislatures is the most formidable dread at present, and will be for many years. That of the executive will come in its turn; but it will be at a remote period. I know there are some among us, who would now establish a monarchy. But they are inconsiderable in number and weight of character. The rising race are all republicans. We were educated in royalism; no wonder, if some of us retain that idolatry still. Our young people are educated in republicanism; an apostasy from that to royalism, is unprecedented and impossible. I am much pleased with the prospect that a declaration of rights will be added; and I hope it will be done in that way, which will not endanger the whole frame of government, or any essential part of it.

To John Adams, June 27, 1813

. . . Men have differed in opinion, and been divided into parties by these opinions, from the first origin of societies, and in all governments where they have been permitted freely to think and to speak. The same political parties which now agitate the United States, have existed through all time. Whether the power of the people or that of the *aristoi* should prevail, were questions which kept the States of Greece and Rome in eternal convulsions, as they now schismatize every people whose minds and mouths are not shut up by the gag of a despot. And in fact, the terms of whig and tory belong to natural as well as to civil history. They denote the temper and constitution of mind of different individuals. To come to our own country, and to the times when you and I became first acquainted, we well remember the violent parties which agitated the old Congress, and their bitter contests. There you and I were together, and the Jays, and the Dickinsons, and other anti-independents, were arrayed against us. They cherished the monarchy of England, and we the rights of our countrymen. When our present government was in the mew, passing from Confederation to Union, how bitter was the schism between the Feds and Antis! Here you and I were together again. For although, for a moment, separated by the Atlantic from the scene of action, I favored the opinion that nine States should confirm the constitution, in order to secure it, and the others hold off until certain amendments, deemed favorable to freedom, should be made. I rallied in the first instant to the wiser proposition of Massachusetts, that all should confirm, and then all instruct their delegates to urge those amendments. The amendments were made, and all were reconciled to the government. But as soon as it was put into motion, the line of division was again drawn. We broke into two parties, each wishing to give the government a different direction; the one to strengthen the most popular branch, the other the more permanent branches, and to extend their permanence. Here you and I separated for the first time, and as we had been longer than most others on the public theatre, and our names therefore were more familiar to our countrymen, the party which considered you as thinking with them, placed your name at their head; the other, for the same reason, selected mine. . . .

To John Adams, October 28, 1813

. . . For I agree with you that there is a natural aristocracy among men. The grounds of this are virtue and talents. Formerly bodily powers gave place among the *aristoi*. But since the invention of gunpowder has armed the weak as well as the strong with missile death, bodily strength, like beauty, good humor, politeness and other accomplishments, has become but an auxiliary ground of distinction. There is also an artifical aristocracy founded on wealth and birth, without either virtue or talents; for with these it would belong to the first class. The natural aristocracy I consider as the most precious gift of nature for the instruction, the trusts, and government of society. And indeed it would have been inconsistent in creation to have formed man for the social state, and not to have provided virtue and wisdom enough to manage the concerns of the society. May we not even say that that form of government is the best which provides the most effectually for a pure selection of these natural *aristoi* into the offices of government? The artificial aristocracy is a mischievous ingredient in government, and provision should be made to prevent its ascendancy. On the question, What is the best provision, you and I differ; but we differ as rational friends, using the free exercise of our own reason, and mutually indulging its errors. *You* think it best to put the Pseudo-*aristoi* into a separate chamber of legislation where they may be hindered from doing mischief by their coordinate branches, and where also they may be a protection to wealth against the Agrarian and plundering enterprises of the Majority of the people. I think that to give them power in order to prevent them from doing mischief, is arming them for it, and increasing instead of remedying the evil. For if the coordinate branches can arrest their action, so may they that of the coordinates. Mischief may be done negatively as well as positively. Of this a cabal in the Senate of the U.S. has furnished many proofs. Nor do I believe them necessary to protect the wealthy; because enough of these will find their way into every branch of the legislation to protect themselves. From 15 to 20 legislatures of our own, in action for 30 years past, have proved that no fears of an equalisation of property are to be apprehended from them.

I think the best remedy is exactly that provided by all our constitutions, to leave to the citizens the free election and separation of the *aristoi* from the pseudo-*aristoi,* of the wheat from the chaff. In general they will elect the real good and wise. In some instances, wealth may corrupt, and birth blind them; but not in sufficient degree to endanger the society.

It is probable that our difference of opinion may in some measure be produced by a difference of character in those among whom we live. From what I have seen of Massachusetts and Connecticut myself, and still more from what I have heard, and the character given of the former by yourself, who know them so much better, there seems to be in those two states a traditionary reverence for certain families, which has rendered the offices of the government nearly hereditary in those families. I presume that from an early period of your history, members of these families happening to possess virtue and talents, have honestly exercised them for the good of the people, and by their services have endeared their names to them.

In coupling Connecticut with you, I mean it politically only, not morally. For having made the Bible the Common law of their land they seem to have modelled their morality on the story of Jacob and Laban. But altho' this hereditary succession to office with you may in some degree be founded in real family merit, yet in a much higher degree it has proceeded from your strict alliance of church and state. These families are canonised in the eyes of the people on the common principle 'you tickle me, and I will tickle you.' In Virginia we have nothing of this. Our clergy, before the revolution, having secured against rivalship by fixed salaries, did not give themselves the trouble of acquiring influence over the people. Of wealth, there were great accumulations in particular families, handed down from generation to generation under the English law of entails. But the only object of ambition for the wealthy was a seat in the king's council. All their court then was paid to the crown and it's creatures; and they Philipised in all collisions between the king and people. Hence they were unpopular; and that unpopularity continues attached to their names. A Randolph, a Carter, or a Burwell must have great personal superiority over a common competitor to be elected by the people, even at this day.

At the first session of our legislature after the Declaration of Independence, we passed a law abolishing entails. And this was followed by one abolishing the privilege of Primogeniture, and dividing the lands of intestates equally among all their children, or other representatives. These laws, drawn by myself, laid the axe to the root of Pseudo-aristocracy. And had another which I prepared been adopted by the legislature, our work would have been compleat. It was a Bill for the more general diffusion of learning. This proposed to divide every county into wards of 5 or 6 miles square, like your townships; to establish in each ward a free school for reading, writing and common arithmetic; to provide for the annual selection of the best subjects from these schools who might receive at the public expense a higher degree of education at a district school; and from these district schools to select a certain number of the most promising subjects to be compleated at an University, where all the useful sciences should be taught. Worth and genius would thus have been sought out from every condition of life, and compleatly prepared by education for defeating the competition of wealth and birth for public trusts.

My proposition had for a further object to impart to these wards those portions of self-government for which they are best qualified, by confiding to them the care of their poor, their roads, police, elections, the nomination of jurors, administration of justice in small cases, elementary exercises of militia, in short, to have made them little republics, with a Warden at the head of each, for all those concerns which, being under their eye, they would better manage than the larger republics of the county or state. A general call of ward-meetings by their Wardens on the same day thro' the state would at any time produce the genuine sense of the people on any required point, and would enable the state to act in mass, as your people have so often done, and with so much effect, by their town meetings. The law for religious freedom, which made a part of this system, having put down the aristocracy of the clergy, and restored to the citizen the freedom of the mind, and those of entails and descents nurturing an equality of condition among them, this on Education would have raised the mass of the people to the high ground of moral respectability necessary to their own safety, and to orderly government; and would have compleated the great object of qualifying them to select the veritable *aristoi,* for the trusts of government, to the exclusion of the Pseudalists: and the same Theognis who has furnished the epigraphs of your two letters assures us that ["Curnis, good men have never harmed any city."] Altho' this law has not yet been acted on but in a small and inefficient degree, it is still considered as before the legislature, with other bills of the revised code, not yet taken up, and I have great hope that some patriotic spirit will, at a favorable moment, call it up, and make it the key-stone of the arch of our government.

With respect to Aristocracy, we should further consider that, before the establishment of the American states, nothing was known to History but the Man of the old World, crouded within limits either small or overcharged, and steeped in the vices which that situation generates. A government adapted to such men would be one thing; but a very different one than for the Man of these states. Here every one may have land to labor for himself if he chuses; or, preferring the exercise of any other industry, may exact for it such compensation as not only to afford a comfortable subsistence, but wherewith to provide for a cessation from labor in old age. Every one, by his property, or by his satisfactory situation, is interested in the support of law and order. And such men may safely and advantageously reserve to themselves a wholesome controul over their public affairs, and a degree of freedom, which in the hands of the Canaille of the cities of Europe, would be instantly perverted to the demolition and destruction of every thing public and private. The history of the last 25 years of France, and of the last 40 years in America, nay of it's last 200 years, proves the truth of both parts of this observation.

But even in Europe a change has sensibly taken place in the mind of Man. Science had liberated the ideas of those who read and reflect, and the American example had kindled feelings of right in the people. An insurrection has consequently begun, of science, talents and courage against rank and birth, which have fallen into contempt. It has failed in it's first effort, because of the mobs of the cities, the instrument used for it's accomplishment, debased by ignorance, poverty and vice, could not be restrained to rational action. But the world will recover from the panic of this first catastrophe. Science is progressive, and talents and enterprize on the alert. Resort may be had to the people of the country, a more governable power from their principles and subordination; and rank, and birth, and tinsel-aristocracy will finally shrink into insignificance, even there. This however we have no right to meddle with. It suffices for us, if the moral and physical condition of our own citizens qualifies them to select the able and good for the direction of their government, with a recurrence of elections at such short periods as will enable them to displace an unfaithful servant before the mischief he meditates may be irremediable. . . .

To Thomas Law, June 13, 1814

. . . To ourselves, in strict language, we can owe no duties, obligation requiring also two parties. Self-love, therefore, is no part of morality. Indeed it is exactly its counterpart. It is the sole antagonist of virtue, leading us constantly by our propensities to self-gratification in violation of our moral duties to others. Accordingly, it is against this enemy that are erected the batteries of moralists and religionists, as the only obstacle to the practice of morality. Take from man his selfish propensities, and he can have nothing to seduce him from the practice of virtue. Or subdue those propensities by education, instruction or restraint, and virtue remains without a competitor. Egoism, in a broader sense, has been thus presented as the source of moral action. It has been said that we feed the hungry, clothe the naked, bind up the wounds of the man beaten by thieves, pour oil and wine into them, set him on our own beast and bring him to the inn, because we receive ourselves pleasure from these acts. . . .

The Creator would indeed have been a bungling artist, had he intended man for a social animal, without planting in him social dispositions. It is true they are not planted in every man, because there is no rule without exceptions; but it is false reasoning which converts exceptions into the general rule. Some men are born without the organs of sight, or of hearing, or without hands. Yet it would be wrong to say that man is born without these faculties, and sight, hearing, and hands may with truth enter into the general definition of man.

The want or imperfection of the moral sense in some men, like the want or imperfection of the senses of sight and hearing in others, is no proof that it is a general characteristic of the species. When it is wanting, we endeavor to supply the defect by education, by appeals to reason and calculation, by presenting to the being so unhappily conformed, other motives to do good and to eschew evil, such as the love, or hatred, or rejection of those among whom he lives, and whose society is necessary to his happiness and even existence; demonstrations by sound calculation that honesty promotes interest in the long run; the rewards and penalties established by the laws; and ultimately the prospects of a future state of retribution for the evil as well as the good done while here. These are the correctives which are supplied by education, and which exercise the functions of the moralist, the preacher, and legislator; and they lead into a course of correct action all those whose disparity is not too profound to be eradicated. Some have argued against the existence of a moral sense, by saying that if nature had given us such a sense, impelling us to virtuous actions, and warning us against those which are vicious, then nature would also have designated, by some particular ear-marks, the two sets of actions which are, in themselves, the one virtuous and the other vicious. Whereas, we find, in fact, that the same actions are deemed virtuous in one country and vicious in another. The answer is, that nature has constituted *utility* to man, the standard and test of virtue. Men living in different countries, under different circumstances, different habits and regimens, may have different utilities; the same act, therefore, may be useful, and consequently virtuous in one country which is injurious and vicious in another differently circumstanced. I sincerely, then, believe with you in the general existence of a moral instinct. I think it the brighest gem with which the human character is studded, and the want of it as more degrading than the most hideous of the bodily deformities. . . .

To Pierre Samuel Dupont de Nemours, April 24, 1816

I received, my dear friend, your letter covering the constitution for your Equinoctial republics. . . . I suppose it well-formed for those for whom it was intended, and the excellence of every government is its adaptation to the state of those to be governed by it. For us it would not do. Distinguishing between the structure of the government and the moral principles on which you prescribe its administration, with the latter we concur cordially, with the former we should not. We of the United States, you know, are constitutionally and conscientiously democrats. We consider society as one of the natural wants with which man has been created; that he has been endowed with faculties and qualities to effect its satisfaction by concurrence of others having the same want; that when, by the exercise of these faculties, he has procured a state of society, it is one of his acquisitions which he has a right to regulate and control, jointly indeed with all those who have concurred in the procurement, whom he cannot exclude from its use or direction more than they him. We think experience has proved it safer, for the mass of individuals composing the society, to reserve to themselves personally the exercise of all rightful powers to which they are competent, and to delegate those to which they are not competent to deputies named, and removable for unfaithful conduct by themselves immediately. Hence, with us, the people (by which is meant the mass of individuals composing the society) being competent to judge of the facts occurring in ordinary life, they have retained the functions of judges of facts under the name of jurors; but being unqualified for the management of affairs requiring intelligence above the common level, yet competent judges of human character, they chose, for their management, representatives, some by themselves immediately, others by electors chosen by themselves. . . .

But when we come to the moral principles on which the government is to be administered, we come to what is proper for all conditions of society. I meet you there in all the benevolence and rectitude of your native character, and I love myself always most where I concur most with you. Liberty, truth, probity, honor are declared to be the four cardinal principles of your society. I believe with you that morality, compassion, generosity are innate elements of the human constitution; that there exists a right independent of force; that a right to property is founded in our natural wants, in the means with which we are endowed to satisfy these wants, and the right to what we acquire by those means without violating the similar rights of other sensible beings; that no one has a right to obstruct another exercising his faculties innocently for the relief of sensibilities made a part of his nature; that justice is the fundamental law of society; that the majority, oppressing an individual, is guilty of a crime, abuses its strength, and by acting on the law of the strongest breaks up the foundations of society; that action by the citizens in person, in affairs within their reach and competence, and in all others by representatives, chosen immediately and removable by themselves, constitutes the essence of a republic; that all governments are more or less republican in proportion as this principle enters more or less into their composition; and that a government by representation is capable of extension over a greater surface of country than one of any other form. These, my friend, are the essentials in which you and I agree; however, in our zeal for their maintenance we may be perplexed and divaricate as to the structure of society most likely to secure them.

In the constitution of Spain, as proposed by the late Cortes, there was a principle entirely new to me and not noticed in yours, that no person born after that day should ever acquire the rights to citizenship until he could read and write. It is impossible sufficiently to estimate the wisdom of this provision. Of all those which have been thought of for securing fidelity in the administration of the government, constant ralliance to the principles of the constitution, and progressive amendments with the progressive advances of the human mind or changes in human affairs, it is the most effectual. Enlighten the people generally, and tyranny and oppressions of body and mind will vanish like evil spirits at the dawn of day. Although I do not with some enthusiasts believe that the human condition will ever advance to such a state of perfection as that there shall no longer be pain or vice in the world, yet I believe it susceptible of much improvement, and most of all in matters of government and religion, and that the diffusion of knowledge among the people is to be the instrument by which it is to be effected.

To John Taylor, May 28, 1816

On my return from a long journey and considerable absence from home, I found here the copy of your "Enquiry into the Principles of our Government," which you had been so kind as to send me; and for which I pray you to accept my thanks.[5] The difficulties of getting new works in our situation, inland and without a single bookstore, are such as had prevented my obtaining a copy before; and letters which had accumulated during my absence, and were calling for answers, have not yet permitted me to give to the whole a thorough reading; yet certain that you and I could not think differently on the fundamentals of rightful government, I was impatient, and availed myself of the intervals of repose from the writing-table, to obtain a cursory idea of the body of the work.

[5]"John Taylor of Carolina" (1753–1824), political writer and U.S. Senator, champion of states' rights, and friend and supporter of Jefferson, had published *An Inquiry into the Principles and Policy of the United States* in 1814.—*Editor*

I see in it much matter for profound reflection; much which should confirm our adhesion, in practice, to the good principles of our Constitution, and fix our attention on what is yet to be made good. The sixth section on the good moral principles of our government, I found so interesting and replete with sound principles, as to postpone my letter-writing to its thorough perusal and consideration. Besides much other good matter, it settles unanswerably the right of instructing representatives, and their duty to obey. The system of banking we have both equally and ever reprobated. I contemplate it as a blot left in all our Constitutions, which, if not covered, will end in their destruction, which is already hit by the gamblers in corruption, and is sweeping away in its progress the fortunes and morals of our citizens. Funding I consider as limited, rightfully, to a redemption of the debt within the lives of a majority of the generation contracting it; every generation coming equally, by the laws of the Creator of the world to the free possession of the earth He made for their subsistence, unincumbered by their predecessors, who, like them, were but tenants for life. You have successfully and completely pulverized Mr. Adams' system of orders, and his opening the mantle of republicanism to every government of laws, whether consistent or not with natural right. Indeed, it must be acknowledged, that the term *republic* is of very vague application in every language. Witness the self-styled republics of Holland, Switzerland, Genoa, Venice, Poland. Were I to assign to this term a precise and definite idea, I would say, purely and simply, it means a government by its citizens in mass, acting directly and personally, according to rules established by the majority; and that every other government is more or less republican, in proportion as it has in its composition more or less of this ingredient of the direct action of the citizens. Such a government is evidently restrained to very narrow limits of space and population. I doubt if it would be practicable beyond the extent of a New England township. The first shade from this pure element, which, like that of pure vital air, cannot sustain life of itself, would be where the powers of the government, being divided, should be exercised each by representatives chosen either *pro hac vice,* or for such short terms as should render secure the duty of expressing the will of their constituents. This I should consider as the nearest approach to a pure republic, which is practicable on a large scale of country or population. And we have examples of it in some of our State Constitutions, which, if not poisoned by priest-craft, would prove its excellence over all mixtures with other elements; and, with only equal doses of poison, would still be the best. Other shades of republicanism may be found in other forms of government, where the executive, judiciary and legislative functions, and the different branches of the latter, are chosen by the people more or less directly, for longer terms of years, or for life, or made hereditary; or where there are mixtures of authorities, some dependent on, and others independent of the people. The further the departure from direct and constant control by the citizens, the less has the government of the ingredient of republicanism; evidently none where the authorities are hereditary, as in France, Venice, etc., or self-chosen, as in Holland; and little, where for life, in proportion as the life continues in being after the act of election.

The purest republican feature in the government of our own State, is the House of Representatives. The Senate is equally so the first year, less the second, and so on. The Executive still less, because not chosen by the people directly. The Judiciary seriously anti-republican, because for life; and the national arm wielded, as you observe, by military leaders, irresponsible but to themselves. Add to this the vicious constitution of our county courts (to whom the justice, the executive administration, the taxation, police, the military appointments of the county, and nearly all our daily concerns are confided), self-appointed, self-continued, holding their authorities for life, and with an impossibility of breaking in on the perpetual succession of any faction once possessed of the bench. They are in truth, the executive, the judiciary, and the military of their respective counties, and the sum of the counties makes the State. And add, also, that one-half of our brethren who fight and pay taxes, are excluded, like Helots, from the rights of representation, as if society were instituted for the soil, and not for the men inhabiting it; or one-half of these could dispose of the rights and the will of the other half, without their consent.

What constitutes a State?
Not high-raised battlements, or labor'd mound,
Thick wall, or moated gate;
Not cities proud, with spires and turrets crown'd;
No: men, high-minded men;
Men, who their duties know;
But know their rights; and knowing, dare maintain.
These constitute a State.

In the General Government, the House of Representatives is mainly republican; the Senate scarcely so at all, as not elected by the people directly, and so long secured even against those who do elect them; the Executive more republican than the Senate, from its shorter term, its election by the people, in *practice,* (for they vote for A only on an assurance that he will vote for B,) and because, *in practice also,* a principle of rotation seems to be in a course of establishment; the judiciary independent of the nation, their coercion by impeachment being found nugatory.

If, then, the control of the people over the organs of their government be the measure of its republicanism, and I confess I know no other measure, it must be agreed that our governments have much less of republicanism than ought to have been expected; in other words, that the people have less regular control over their agents, than their rights and their interests require. And this I ascribe, not to any want of republican dispositions in those who formed these Constitutions, but to a submission of true principle to European authorities, to speculators on government, whose fears of the people have been inspired by the populace of their own great cities, and were unjustly entertained against the independent, the happy, and therefore orderly citizens of the United States. Much I apprehend that the golden moment is past for reforming these heresies. The functionaries of public power rarely strengthen in their dispositions to abridge it, and an unorganized call for timely amendment is not likely to prevail against an organized opposition to it. We are always told that things are going on well; why change them? *"Chista bene, non si muove,"* said the Italian, "let him who stands well, stand still." This is true; and I verily believe they would go on well with us under an absolute monarch, while our present character remains, of order, industry and love of peace, and restrained, as he would be, by the proper spirit of the people. But it is while it remains such, we should provide against the consequences of its deterioration. And let us rest in the hope that it will yet be done, and spare ourselves the pain of evils which may never happen.

On this view of the import of the term *republic,* instead of saying, as has been said, "that it may mean anything or nothing," we may say with truth and meaning, that governments are more or less republican, as they have more or less of the element of popular election and control in their composition; and believing, as I do, that the mass of the citizens is the safest depository of their own rights and especially, that the evils flowing from the duperies of the people, are less injurious than those from the egoism of their agents, I am a friend to that composition of government which has in it the most of this ingredient. And I sincerely believe, with you, that banking establishments are more dangerous than standing armies; and that the principle of spending money to be paid by posterity, under the name of funding, is but swindling futurity on a large scale. . . .

To Isaac H. Tiffany, August 26, 1816

. . . But so different was the style of society then and with those people from what it is now and with us that I think little edification can be obtained from their writings on the subject of government.[6] They had just ideas of the value of personal liberty, but none at all of the structure of government best calculated to preserve it. They knew no medium between a democracy (the only pure republic, but impracticable beyond the limits of a town) and an abandonment of themselves to an aristocracy or a tyranny independent of the people. It seems not to have occurred that where the citizens cannot meet to transact their business in person, they alone have the right to choose the agents who shall transact it; and that in this way a republican or popular government of the second grade of purity may be exercised over any extent of country. The full experiment of a government democratical

[6]Jefferson refers to the ancient Greeks, and his comment is on Aristotle's *Politics.—Editor*

but representative was and is still reserved for us. The idea, (taken, indeed, from the little specimen formerly existing in the English constitution but now lost) has been carried by us more or less into all our legislative and executive departments; but it has not yet by any of us been pushed into all the ramifications of the system, so far as to leave no authority existing not responsible to the people, whose rights, however, to the exercise and fruits of their own industry can never be protected against the selfishness of rulers not subject to their control at short periods. The introduction of this new principle of representative democracy has rendered useless almost everything written before on the structure of government, and in a great measure relieves our regret if the political writings of Aristotle or of any other ancient have been lost or are unfaithfully rendered or explained to us. My most earnest wish is to see the republican element of popular control pushed to the maximum of its practicable exercise. I shall then believe that our government may be pure and perpetual.

To Samuel Kercheval, July 12, 1816

I am not among those who fear the people. They, and not the rich, are our dependence for continued freedom. And to preserve their independence, we must not let our rulers load us with perpetual debt. We must make our election between *economy and liberty,* or *profusion and servitude.* If we run into such debts, as that we must be taxed in our meat and in our drink, in our necessaries and our comforts, in our labors and our amusements, for our callings and our creeds, as the people of England are, our people, like them, must come to labor sixteen hours in the twenty-four, give the earnings of fifteen of these to the government for their debts and daily expenses; and the sixteenth being insufficient to afford us bread, we must live, as they now do, on oatmeal and potatoes; have no time to think, no means of calling the mismanagers to account; but be glad to obtain subsistence by hiring ourselves to rivet their chains on the necks of our fellow sufferers. Our landholders, too, like theirs, retaining indeed the title and stewardship of estates called theirs, but held really in trust for the treasury, must wander, like theirs, in foreign countries, and be contented with penury, obscurity, exile, and the glory of the nation. This example reads to us the salutary lesson, that private fortunes are destroyed by public as well as by private extravagance. And this is the tendency of all human governments. A departure from principle in one instance becomes a precedent for a second; that second for a third; and so on, till the bulk of the society is reduced to be mere automatons of misery, to have no sensibilities left but for sinning and suffering. Then begins, indeed, the *bellum omnium in omnia,* which some philosophers observing to be so general in this world, have mistaken it for the natural, instead of the abusive state of man. And the fore horse of this frightful team is public debt. Taxation follows that, and in its train wretchedness and oppression.

Some men look at constitutions with sanctimonious reverence, and deem them like the ark of the convenant, too sacred to be touched. They ascribe to the men of the preceding age a wisdom more than human, and suppose what they did to be beyond amendment. I knew that age well; I belonged to it, and labored with it. It deserved well of its country. It was very like the present, but without the experience of the present; and forty years of experience in government is worth a century of bookreading; and this they would say themselves, were they to rise from the dead. I am certainly not an advocate for frequent and untried changes in laws and constitutions. I think moderate imperfections had better be borne with; because, when once known, we accommodate ourselves to them, and find practical means of correcting their ill effects. But I know also, that laws and institutions must go hand in hand with the progress of the human mind. As that becomes more developed, more enlightened, as new discoveries are made, new truths disclosed, and manners and opinions change with the change of circumstances, institutions must advance also, and keep pace with the times. We might as well require a man to wear still the coat which fitted him when a boy, as civilized society to remain ever under the regimen of their barbarous ancestors. It is this preposterous idea which has lately deluged Europe in blood. Their monarchs, instead of wisely yielding to the gradual change of circumstances, of favoring progressive accommodation to progressive improvement, have clung to old abuses, entrenched themselves behind steady habits, and obliged their subjects to seek through blood and violence rash and ruinous innovations, which, had they been referred to the peaceful deliberations and collected wisdom of the nation, would have been put into acceptable and salutary forms. Let us follow no such examples, nor weakly believe that one generation is not as capable as another of taking care of itself, and of ordering its own affairs. Let us, as our States have done, avail ourselves of our reason and experience, to correct the crude essays of our first and unexperienced, although wise, virtuous, and well-meaning councils. And lastly, let us provide in our Constitution for its revision at stated periods. What these periods should be, nature herself indicates. By the European tables of mortality, of the adults living at any one moment of time, a majority will be dead in about nineteen years. At the end of that period then, a new majority is come into place; or, in other words, a new generation. Each generation is as independent of the one preceding, as that was of all which had gone before. It has then, like them, a right to choose for itself the form of government it believes most promotive of its own happiness; consequently, to accommodate to the circumstances in which it finds itself, that received from its predecessors; and it is for the peace and good of mankind, that a solemn opportunity of doing this every nineteen or twenty years, should be provided by the Constitution; so that it may be handed on, with periodical repairs, from generation to generation, to the end of time, if anything human can so long endure. It is now forty years since the constitution of Virginia was formed. The same tables inform us, that, within that period, two-thirds of the adults then living are now dead. Have then the remaining third, even if they had the wish, the right to hold in obedience to their will and to laws theretofore made by them, the other two-thirds, who, with themselves, compose the present mass of adults? If they have not, who has? The dead? But the dead have no rights. They are nothing; and nothing cannot own something. Where there is no substance, there can be no accident. This corporeal globe, and everything upon it belong to its present corporeal inhabitants, during their generation. They alone have a right to direct what is the concern of themselves alone, and to declare the law of that direction; and this declaration can only be made by their majority.

That majority, then, has a right to depute representatives to a convention, and to make the Constitution what they think will be the best for themselves. But how collect their voice? This is the real difficulty. If invited by private authority, or county or district meetings, these divisions are so large that few will attend; and their voice will be imperfectly, or falsely, pronounced. Here, then, would be one of the advantages of the ward divisions I have proposed. The mayor of every ward, on a question like the present, would call his ward together, take the simple yea or nay of its members, convey these to the county court, who would hand on those of all its wards to be the proper general authority; and the voice of the whole people would be thus fairly, fully, and peaceably expressed, discussed, and decided by the common reason of the society. If this avenue be shut to the call of sufferance, it will make itself heard through that of force, and we shall go on, as other nations are doing, in the endless circle of oppression, rebellion, reformation; and oppression, rebellion, reformation, again; and so on forever. . . .

To John Holmes, April 22, 1820

I thank you, dear Sir, for the copy you have been so kind as to send me of the letter to your constituents on the Missouri question.[7] It is a perfect justification to them. I had for a long time ceased to read newspapers, or pay any attention to public affairs, confident they were in good hands, and content to be a passenger in our bark to the shore from which I am not distant. But this momentous question, like a fire-bell in the night, awakened and filled me with terror. I considered it at once as the knell of the Union. It is hushed, indeed, for the moment. But this is a reprieve only, not a final sentence. A geographical line, coinciding with a marked principle, moral and political, once conceived and held up

[7]The "Missouri question" concerning slavery was resolved for a time by the Missouri Compromise (1820) by which Missouri was admitted as a slave state, Maine as a free state, and slavery was prohibited in the territories above the latitude 36°30'. Jefferson vehemently disapproved of it on the ground that party differences would become fixed as sectional differences and thus endanger the union.—*Editor*

to the angry passions of men, will never be obliterated; and every new irritation will mark it deeper and deeper. I can say, with conscious truth, that there is not a man on earth who would sacrifice more than I would to relieve us from this heavy reproach, in any *practicable* way. The cession of that kind of property, for so it is misnamed, is a bagatelle which would not cost me a second thought, if, in that way, a general emancipation and *expatriation* could be effected; and, gradually, and with due sacrifices, I think it might be. But as it is, we have the wolf by the ears, and we can neither hold him, nor safely let him go. Justice is in one scale, and self-preservation in the other. Of one thing I am certain, that as the passage of slaves from one State to another, would not make a slave of a single human being who would not be so without it, so their diffusion over a greater surface would make them individually happier, and proportionally facilitate the accomplishment of their emancipation, by dividing the burden on a greater number of coadjutors. An abstinence too, from this act of power, would remove the jealousy excited by the undertaking of Congress to regulate the condition of the different descriptions of men composing a State. This certainly is the exclusive right of every State, which nothing in the Constitution has taken from them and given to the General Government. Could Congress, for example, say that the non-freemen of Connecticut shall be freemen, or that they shall not emigrate into any other State?

I regret that I am now to die in the belief, that the useless sacrifice of themselves by the generation of 1776, to acquire self-government and happiness to their country, is to be thrown away by the unwise and unworthy passions of their sons, and that my only consolation is to be, that I live not to weep over it. If they would but dispassionately weigh the blessings they will throw away, against an abstract principle more likely to be effected by union than by scission, they would pause before they would perpetrate this act of suicide on themselves, and of treason against the hopes of the world. To yourself, as the faithful advocate of the Union, I tender the offering of my high esteem and respect.

selected bibliography

Jefferson's works

Boyd, Julian P. and others, eds. *The Papers of Thomas Jefferson*, 19 vols. to date. Princeton, N.J.: 1950–1974.

Cappon, Lester J., ed. *The Adams-Jefferson Letters*, 2 vols. Chapel Hill, N.C.: 1959.

Dumbauld, Edward, ed. *The Political Writings of Thomas Jefferson*. New York, 1955.

Ford, Paul L., ed. *The Writings of Thomas Jefferson*, 10 vols. New York, 1892–1899.

Lipscomb, A. A. and A. E. Bergh, eds. *The Writings of Thomas Jefferson*, 20 vols. Washington, 1903.

Peden, William, ed. *Notes on the State of Virginia*. Chapel Hill, N.C.: 1955.

books and articles on Jefferson

Adair, Douglass. *Fame and the Founding Fathers*. New York, 1974.

Adams, Henry. *History of the United States During the Administrations of Jefferson and Madison*, 9 vols. New York, 1891–1893.

Becker, Carl. *The Declaration of Independence*. New York, 1922.

Boorstin, Daniel J. *The Lost World of Thomas Jefferson*. New York, 1948.

Brann, Eva. "Concerning the declaration of independence." *The College* (St John's College, Annapolis, Maryland). July, 1976, pp. 1–17.

Brodie, Fawn M. *Thomas Jefferson, An Intimate History*. New York, 1974.

Cunningham, Noble E., Jr. *The Jeffersonian Republicans, The Formation of Party Organization, 1789–1802*. Chapel Hill, N.C.: 1957.

Jaffa, Harry V. "Agrarian Virtue and Republican Freedom: An Historical Perspective" in Jaffa, *Equality and Freedom* New York, 1965, pp. 42–66.

Jaffa, Harry V. "The Virtue of a Nation of Cities: On the Jeffersonian Paradoxes" in Jaffa, *The Conditions of Freedom* Baltimore, 1975, pp. 99–110.

Koch, Adrienne. *The Philosophy of Thomas Jefferson.* New York, 1943.

Koch, A. and W. Peden. *The Life and Selected Writings of Thomas Jefferson.* New York, 1944.

Lee, Henry. *Observations on the Writings of Thomas Jefferson.* Philadelphia, 1839.

Levy, Leonard. *Jefferson and Civil Liberties: The Darker Side.* Cambridge, Mass., 1963.

Malone, Dumas. *Jefferson and His Time,* 5 vols. Boston: 1948–1974.

Merriam, Charles E. "The Political Theory of Jefferson," *Political Science Quarterly,* XVII (March, 1902), pp. 24–45.

Peterson, Merrill D. *The Jefferson Image in the American Mind.* New York, 1960.

Peterson, Merrill D., ed. *Thomas Jefferson: A Profile.* New York, 1967.

Peterson, Merrill D. *Jefferson and the New Nation: A Biography.* New York, 1970.

White, Leonard D. *The Jeffersonians: A Study in Administrative History, 1801–1829.* New York, 1951.

Wiltse, Charles M. *The Jeffersonian Tradition in American Democracy.* Chapel Hill, N.C.: 1951.